Boston Tea Party

The Shocking Event That Triggered the American Revolution

(A Modern Editorial on the Boston Tea Party)

Gerald Scoggins

Published By **Bella Frost**

Gerald Scoggins

All Rights Reserved

Boston Tea Party: The Shocking Event That Triggered the American Revolution (A Modern Editorial on the Boston Tea Party)

ISBN 978-1-7771462-0-7

No part of this guidebook shall be reproduced in any form without permission in writing from the publisher except in the case of brief quotations embodied in critical articles or reviews.

Legal & Disclaimer

The information contained in this book is not designed to replace or take the place of any form of medicine or professional medical advice. The information in this book has been provided for educational & entertainment purposes only.

The information contained in this book has been compiled from sources deemed reliable, and it is accurate to the best of the Author's knowledge; however, the Author cannot guarantee its accuracy and validity and cannot be held liable for any errors or omissions. Changes are periodically made to this book. You must consult your doctor or get professional medical advice before using any of the suggested remedies, techniques, or information in this book.

Upon using the information contained in this book, you agree to hold harmless the Author from and against any damages, costs, and expenses, including any legal fees potentially resulting from the application of any of the information provided by this guide. This disclaimer applies to any damages or injury caused by the use and application, whether directly or indirectly, of any advice or information presented, whether for breach of contract, tort, negligence, personal injury, criminal intent, or under any other cause of action.

You agree to accept all risks of using the information presented inside this book. You need to consult a professional medical practitioner in order to ensure you are both able and healthy enough to participate in this program.

Table Of Contents

Chapter 1: The Customs House 1

Chapter 2: The Boston Massacre 11

Chapter 3: Apprenticeship 32

Chapter 4: The Tavern........................... 48

Chapter 5: The Plan............................... 73

Chapter 6: The Gaspee Affair 85

Chapter 7: A Second Massacre Averted . 97

Chapter 8: An Arrest 110

Chapter 9: The Tea Act......................... 122

Chapter 10: The Hutchinson 134

Chapter 11: Jail 147

Chapter 12: Boston Tea Party 160

Chapter 13: Epilogue........................... 174

Chapter 1: The Customs House

The air was acrid the air was soaring as Samuel Maverick headed through Boston right, aiming to make it at Isaac Carrey's residence. The snow was just beginning to melt and the air was infused with it a warm, cosy feel which had not been present for several months.

This was why it was that the streets were filled with crowds. People were gathering around talking about recent happenings that had occurred in the city. This was not unusual However, what was unique was the sense of anger and frustration Samuel was able to sense within the crowd.

Samuel was trying to avoid getting involved in anything which was taking place. His boss, Isaac Greenwood, had said that it was the best thing to do.

"A young man such as yourself needs to keep his head down and concentrate on learning your trade. Don't go borrowing trouble, and just keep out of things. You'll have plenty of time to get involved in politics when you're grown and established."

Samuel was determined to take the advice of his boss, however it was tough to keep track of the events that were taking place in the city as well as in the country surrounding it. He didn't want to do was risk his place with the Greenwood family. It was imperative to understand the art of trading, but he was unsure of where to get another job in the event that it was lost that was at the Greenwoods'.

It seemed that there was every day British soldiers out in the open. The soldiers did to make it work with the colonists. However, some seemed unhappy the fact that they were stationed in Boston. They looked at Bostonians from Boston as if they were impoverished like Boston was an unclean small, unclean little town instead of a more sophisticated city.

Every time Samuel was in a shopping mall and walked into a store, he could tell that those who were there were discussing nothing but the cost of products that were coming to the store from outside. As Samuel was with his boss around the table to eat dinner later in the evening The Greenwoods spoke about the difficulty to earn profits. The amount of anger expressed in the comments of others had risen in the past in the town, which caused it to look like a massive pot of powder waiting to explode.

A few nights ago, at dinner Samuel's employer was discussing the issue with his family and wife. "Ever since those damned Townshend Acts were brought about its so expensive to buy anything from overseas," Isaac Greenwood said. Isaac Greenwood. "If it's not one tax, it's another. Those damned Brits are finding a way to suck us dry of every last bit of money. I hate to raise my prices but after trying to deal with how much everything costs, I don't see as I have much of a choice." All of them had nodded their heads in to each other in agreement. Taxes that were high imposed through Townshend Acts Townshend Acts had definitely impacted their businesses. Every person at the table thought about how bad things would be.

Samuel turned his head in a bid to think about the direction he was heading to. Samuel looked around to find the exact location he was. Samuel was walking towards the road which was where the Carrey family resided. The home was located in an area that was lively. There was a Tavern situated on King Street, and on warm evenings, live entertainment and music would often spill onto the streets. A little further down King Street there was a customs house, which was always a source of energy and fun. Samuel generally didn't spend any time for himself during the late evenings. He was always mastering his trade, and he most of the money was made to his mom and brother.

This evening, Samuel had been invited to dinner at the Carrey home. Some of his friends were expected to gather at the residence and it was expected to be a great evening. Mrs. Carrey was an excellent cook and enjoyed her job of making sure the boys her son was a friend with enjoyed a delicious meal and had fun.

Five people were present on the night before; among the group was Isaac Greenwood Junior as well as Isaac's brother John. Everyone was engaged in the process of making their meal when the ring were rung. Samuel is the one one to be able to hear the sound. The sounds were muffled by the walls however, as it grew more and more loud, it was impossible to not hear.

"Are those fire bells?" Samuel asked. Samuel.

Isaac John Greenwood and John Greenwood looked up. After listening, Isaac looked uncertain. "I'm not sure, to be honest." Isaac is no familiar with fire alarms. There were a good amount of fires that had occurred in this region of the city, however it seemed like this was different. "I think we need to go out and see what is going on."

Samuel looked around in the kitchen. He saw the Mrs. Carrey had a worried expression in her eyes. Prior to her having an opportunity to express her thoughts to them The group of youngsters walked out of the front door, and then followed by the other group of individuals moving towards King Street.

In the beginning, it was hard to discern the situation. The sun was setting and the streets were filled with long shadows however the large number of people going towards one direction was making easy for Samuel and his family members which direction the sound was coming from. When Samuel's party approached the intersection, they could spot a bigger crowd gathered near the Customs House. As they moved closer towards the crowd they could glimpse the bright red of British soldiers in the distance.

Although the sight of redcoats was not unusual however, Samuel was shivering up his spine.

The bells were ringing, and a high pitched rumble could be heard out of the crowd. Samuel and his companions were too far from where they could hear the conversation, however the crowd seemed to be agitated and it was not clear if that things would calm anytime soon.

Samuel and his fellows stared at each other. They started to move more and more quickly. They soon were being pulled through the crowd. The crowd of people surrounding the group was rapidly turning into a raged crowd. They'd been battling the British for many years, paying taxes after tax, that they were exhausted. They finally had an chance to express their anger The crowd arranged to do it.

March 5, 1770

Chapter 2: The Boston Massacre

Samuel turned to his fellows. "I'm going to move up and see what is happening. This doesn't look good."

This certainly wasn't the look of the kind of fire that would be seen. Samuel took his time getting toward the center of the crowd. There was seven soldiers gathering at the front of the customs building. They seemed a bit nervous and Samuel did not seem to be shocked.

A few of them have clearly been practicing the same thing for longer, carrying their muskets at an confidence. Some looked as if this was their first time in the field and weren't sure how to deal with the crowd of angry colonists that were gathered in front. Samuel was looking to his left as a man of middle age began shouting on the soldier.

"You damn lobsterbacks! Get out of our city! Don't you know you're not wanted here? Get out and let decent folk get back to living their lives!" Samuel was able to recognize the person.

This was one of the most loyal customers of his company. He had been adamant with Isaac Greenwood Senior regarding the tax burden that drove up the cost of furniture Isaac Samuel and Samuel made for him.

"Yes! Get out! Get out of our city!" A number of people yelled. They started to move ahead, drawing onwards towards the soldiers. Samuel noticed that he was being pulled into the air.

After that, he felt a bang and observed one soldier look a bit uncomfortable and then turn toward the opposite. A person began throwing snowballs.

"A snowball's not enough! Kill them! Grab their muskets! Teach the lobsterbacks what happens when they go somewhere they aren't wanted!" The last time, the sound which rang out was from an individual farther back from the crowd.

Another voice spoke. "Yes! Kill them! If we don't, they'll just come back. Kill them now!" The snowballs, chunks of mud and handful of stones were hurled at soldiers. The filthy snow washed into their brilliant red jackets. Younger soldiers started to gaze at older members of their division, waiting for an indication of the best way to respond.

Samuel took a look at the faces of the crowd, and attempted to identify his companions. Samuel couldn't. He felt that the occupants were hanging farther from him than they were. Samuel was being pulled to the front. The soldiers had retreated somewhat, but it was evident that they were not going to get out of the way in front of the Customs House. The only limit was the distance they could push. Samuel didn't know how much further pushing could do.

He was aware of the anger in the crowd. He was sick of seeing soldiers pacing in the streets of his town as well. Samuel had not seen them do any good or helping. Their presence in the area only meant an increase in taxes and trouble to good, law-abiding employees like his employer. As soon as they left then the faster life can return normal. The snowballs continued to flutter and the mud poured out. They raised their muskets before aiming at the people. They reacted furiously.

"Fire away, you damned lobsterbacks!" shouted Samuel by raising his arm and raising his fist up in the air. "Fire away if you have the courage!" A snowball landed on the musket of the young soldier. Samuel saw it fall to the floor.

Within a few seconds after, the British soldier picked it back up. His expression had changed from one of trepidation into one that was filled with anger and determination.

Samuel observed the soldiers giving each other a final glance before shots began to ring out. Samuel was puzzled as to why soldiers were shooting when they were told not to. wasn't yet given. The smoke was erupting from the horizon and Samuel heard his ears vibrate. The air was scented with burned powder. He was right next with the troops. The two muskets that had been fired first were pointed at the centre of the group with screams heard emanating from different locations within the crowd. And then, all of a sudden, the person closest to Samuel was shot. He didn't initially notice any sensation.

He then felt the sensation. The musket ball smashed into his body then Samuel took hold of his shoulder. Samuel could hear soldiers yelling at one another as well as crying and screaming from the mass of people.

He turned his back and observed that the road was becoming empty. There were a few lying on the floor, unable to move. They were not to be found. Everyone was fleeing in different directions. There was no sentiment of being together completely gone. Samuel attempted to sprint however he was unable to do so. His body felt dry and warm. He ran down an alley on his left and walked as fast as was possible. The warm smudge that was on his shirt was growing. Samuel took a look at his hands and was stunned to find it was covered in blood. The blood was so thick.

Samuel sat against the side of the building, and tried to breathe. The black spots glowed across his face and he sank into a sitting posture. He leaned his head to the structure and tried to think of ways to escape the hole he found himself stuck in.

It was a bit gruelling. Samuel only needed to make it to the Carrey home. Samuel felt certain his companions would've retreated in the back and hoped they were wondering what transpired to the man. Samuel attempted to rise on his feet, but was unable to. He moaned and was able to sink back in a reclined posture. It felt almost like a comfortable position was all he needed to do was cease to hurt. Samuel shut his eyes and hoped some one, or anyone, was able to find him and aid to get him back on track.

It could turn out to be an extremely long and painful night.

March-December, 1770 Awaiting the Trial

Jacob was able to recall the look of his mother as she discovered that Samuel had passed away. What a pale, quiet face she was. Jacob was present the moment Samuel's employer came to the house, with his face worried and agitated. His mother had to take Jacob to a different room as she was able to tell Mister Greenwood had to say would be a disaster However, Jacob was able to be able to hear them speaking from the walls.

Her mother was crying at one point, a lengthy broken, heartbroken sound which he'd not ever heard before. The hope was that he'd not hear that sound again. Jacob's father was dead several years before in the past, and Jacob was convinced that his mother might be making a similar sound after hearing about her husband's death. A few years later, Samuel had been the bright spot in her life. The money he earned through his job and the funds which he was able return to his family members had allowed them to cover their expenses and to put an amount of food into their stomachs. Jacob realized that Mother probably felt anxious and scared after hearing that Samuel was deceased.

He was shot dead when the British soldier killed his stomach. Jacob realized that Samuel was not the only one to be killed, and Samuel did not die immediately. The group of people Samuel was amongst had been dispersed and Samuel was abandoned, bleeding into the streets. His friends that he was with left him behind as they tried to run off. According to what Mr. Greenwood told him, Samuel had lain there for several hours and had loosened many a pound of blood. When they finally been able to locate the man and transport the doctor to see him the patient was close to dying. The musket ball's removal was what killed him.

"Here are Samuel's final wages. I was able to add a little extra in there for you. The boy did good work. He was good with both of my sons, Mrs. Maverick. I know that my son John is devastated about Samuel's death. They shared a room, you know. He was good to my children and good to me." Mr. Greenwood went silent following that and all that rang out heard was the mother of Jacob's crying. When she was done, she didn't seem to be absconding, Mister Greenwood spoke again.

"Here is where you can find his body. You'll have to make arrangements shortly. I'm sorry, Missus. I wish there was more that I could do for you and your son. As I say, Samuel was good to me and my family." Then, Jacob heard the door shut and open, and he and his mom were all alone.

Jacob was able to see Isaac Greenwood again a few weeks later, when he took his mother along to collect the items which Samuel had left at Mr. Greenwood's. There was nothing much.

There were a few items Samuel was doing to improve his abilities. A few pieces of clothing. His mother was delighted to know that Mister Greenwood had been willing to donate Samuel's items. Greenwood's son, who was younger than him, brought the items for Jacob as well as his mom. Jacob was like the parents did. John Samuel and John Samuel were in the same room and had become extremely intimate.

"Are you Samuel's brother?" John Greenwood asked Jacob, his voice cracking a bit as he pronounced Samuel's name. Jacob did not respond, he was reluctant to even try speaking. Jacob knew that it would be a challenge to communicate.

"We shared a room, you know. He was good to me. I was so used to having someone in the same room with me and now I'm all alone." John's voice trembled. "When I wake up in the early morning, I look around. I see him sometimes, I think, there in the dark. It's nice when I do. I don't feel so alone that way." John left and went back to his bedroom. Jacob realized that John was attempting to cover his tears. crying.

The following weeks after Samuel's demise were very dark actually. Jacob's mother was barely in a position to survive when she earned Samuel's wage however, when Samuel died, the situation was much more dire. He and his family were forced to leave their house and move into the rooms of an accommodation home. His mother managed to get work cleaning and making repairs, but it was not a great pay and often they'd be hungry. Jacob was able to get odd jobs from time to time however, at the age of fifteen the age of his youth was not yet established and had little to do. Jacob ran around and carried parcels to women shopping. He didn't offer assistance to wives of British soldiers, however. No one would. Everybody living in Boston was a bit displeased with the fact that they were there.

Jacob's mother had stopped speaking to him. Prior to the time that Samuel was murdered the mother had been singing and humming. The Mavericks were not financially secure, however the widow Maverick was always able to find ways to make the situation appear good. Following the death of Samuel passed away, however things changed. It was as if she grew old in a matter of minutes, and she moved at a slower pace. She was less smiling. Jacob was able to tell that she was missing her brother. Jacob was aware of this, as Samuel was missing him too. Samuel also.

In the months that followed, they remained looking forward to hearing that soldiers had been executed. This wasn't only Jacob as well as his mother, everyone in Boston appeared to be waiting on their breath, waiting to hear what might take place. The soldiers were indicted immediately after the incident however, they remained awaiting their trial. The incident may not bring Samuel or any other soldiers who had died to life again however it could be an event.

Jacob was listening to his mom discuss the matter with a neighbors. "There was no order to fire. They were just standing there. That soldier should never have fired. I know that the crowd was shouting at them, but the soldiers could have reacted a different way. Instead, they cut those people down, and they died. My son died."

"I want you to be careful whenever you have to go out, Jacob," his mother advised Jacob. "I want you to keep far away from any British soldiers you see. People aren't being kind to them or their families. Things are getting worse here and I don't want you tangled up in any of the trouble that's going on. I couldn't bear to have anything happen to you; not after what happened to your brother." The mother's face appeared to swell up as it always did when she spoke of Samuel.

It was clear that things were getting worse. Jacob frequently walked past groups of people who gathered in front of anyone who wore the British uniform, yelling at those wearing it and, in some situations, throwing dirt at those wearing the uniforms. Everywhere he went at, he saw his brother as well as the other victims who were killed. The bright blood in red, and also the vivid blood red coloration of British uniforms. The red color caused him to feel sick every time the color was seen.

Then, nine months following the attack The Grand Jury announced what was going to happen for the troops. Jacob was in attendance to witness the verdict. The trial began just a couple of weeks prior in November's final days, and to match the mood in the city it was dark and gray, and snow was already beginning to begin to fall. It seemed like the trial would last forever. When he went out around the area, Jacob heard people talking about the trial.

"It was clear who was at fault. Those damn lobsterbacks opened fire on innocent people," claimed one person in the night. "If one of us had raised a hand to any of them the trial wouldn't have taken near as long." The crowd which had formed close to him were nodding and were muttering with acceptance.

On the night of the sentence Jacob's mother taken him to the market to find work, so they could make a few dollars of money to buy dinner. However, he snuck out and walked into the Courthouse. The mother of Jacob was so active these days, she barely noticed that Jacob left. He didn't have any place to go. Jacob was unable to locate a location where the apprenticeship could begin as well as he was not attending any of the colleges located in the city. Therefore, Jacob managed to sneak inside the courthouse and watch the trial that was currently underway.

When he arrived, Jacob heard the Patriot John Adams describing his brother as being a part of the rabble. He also said that the soldiers were entitled to an obligation to protect themselves. Jacob knew things would not go as planned. He understood that he was an infant, yet it was a shock to hear how passionately John Adams defended the British soldiers.

Following John Adam's energetic talk, Jacob knew that the soldiers would be cleared. He was a genius and both he and his legal assistants had a gift in arguing legal issues. The end result was that Jacob had been right. The soldiers killed his brother with cold blood and not a single person from the group would ever get a full and complete punishment. Jacob's brother's fate did not matter in the least. The Brits could have done whatever they wanted with the colonists and no one Jacob could do to stop the matter. At least, not yet.

There was a rage in the air at the time that soldiers were convicted, with shouting in the courtroom while lawyers debated and the convicts were reading in the Bible.

Jacob was unable to comprehend how this occurred. Six of the soldiers cleared and only two were convicted of manslaughter? Jacob wasn't too surprised to learn that the Brits got off without a hitch however he was unable to comprehend the process of having been found guilty of manslaughter, to being branded with a thumb without serving any jail time. While the agony his soldiers suffered while their sentences were carried out seemed great Five men as well as his brother were murdered, in the end, so it was Jacob thought, all was going to be right in this world once more.

February, 1772

Chapter 3: Apprenticeship

Jacob, are you able to get all your belongings in order?" His mother was speaking to him through the front door. Jacob looked at the little pile of belongings brought with him to the new house he was moving into. He was anxious. As soon as he was out of the space, the rest of his life was going to take the opposite direction. He left to start an apprenticeship with his own.

"Jacob," his mother repeated "Mister Wagner is here to get you." Jacob could feel her footsteps moving towards the bedroom. "You need to make sure that you don't keep him waiting. Remember, how you do at the Wagner's will either help assure you of a good future or hold you back. Hurry up, work hard, and make sure he is happy with your work." The door was leaned against her and Jacob was able to see her eyes start to sparkle slightly more brightly than they did before. Jacob knew exactly the thoughts she was having. He had sent her brother away around the same age, and couple of years after, she lost the boy. Jacob was her all to offer her, and she was now sending her son away, too.

"Mother, I'm all ready to go. I just don't have that much to bring with me, is all." Jacob took a backpack and started to pack his things into it. He wasn't sure what sort of house he'd stay in. Samuel had had a good fortune. The Master of his house had permitted him to stay with his family and offered him a cozy place to live, but there was no guarantee that Jacob could have the same arrangement.

Jacob certainly didn't want to hold his new employer in the dark. He was not going to let Thomas fall down anyhow. Jacob was very lucky in securing this job.

Jacob had been able to get some jobs from time to time making errands and running for Samuel's previous employer. When Isaac Greenfield had already taken another apprentice but had no job to offer Jacob but he did made a positive impression to his acquaintance Thomas Wagner. After Thomas told him the need for an honest, hard-working person to enter the company, Isaac Greenwood had put Jacob's name in the conversation.

Jacob was later informed that the two had debated over the possibility that Master Wagner would take his place. "He's already seventeen, Isaac, why hasn't he started his apprenticeship with someone yet? You know how some boys are at that age. They want to have fun and lark about. They don't want to buckle down and learn."

Jacob did not know exactly what Isaac had said to his friend, however it was clear that in some way Jacob was able to convince Thomas to accept Jacob to the next level and Jacob was certain that he'd be eternally thankful. At first, Jacob knew that he was just working to cover the cost of his accommodation and food. It wasn't atypical. However, as time passed the boy would have the ability to pay home cash just as Samuel did, and was eager assist his mom in need.

"Mother, what are your plans once I go?" Jacob had asked his mom at least a couple of times when discovering that Thomas took the boy on. He had avoided answering his son's questions. Jacob realized the fact that having him in her home and having another feeding a mouth, would be cost-effective. Her struggle was to survive. One of the last things Jacob did was make her feel any discomfort. Her pride was evident and her son understood she did not like asking for assistance from anyone even when she was able to avoid the issue.

"Oh, I have a room lined up. It's not quite as large as this one but I can work and pay for room and board," she smiled, a little. "Now that I don't have to worry about my growing boy I can take on a position like that. Between room and board and any money you eventually send back I should be able to set myself up comfortably." She was able to see the expression on the face of her son. "Oh, Jacob, this is a good thing for us. I've never needed anything lavish or grand. I'm just so pleased that you are getting a good position and learning a trade."

His mother leaned in and embraced him. She and then took his bag. She carried it from another room and towards the front door, at which Jacob discovered his new employer waiting to greet his arrival. Thomas had only seen Thomas at least once, however, he always appeared to be a nice man even if he was a bit in the middle. Jacob has visited his work space periodically to pick up things often and seemed slightly amazed by the sheer size. There were several older men doing work and it was apparent that no one was as big as Jacob with his size and their age.

This was the one thing that made Jacob somewhat down. In the past, when Samuel was a student with the Greenwoods they had Isaac Junior for companionship and also had a roommate was able to talk to. Jacob knew beforehand that once it came time to move into his Wagner home, he'd most likely be by himself. The sacrifice was worth it however, being capable of helping his mom.

Jacob got up on the rear of the wagon pulled by Thomas. When he got up from the bedroom, his mom handed Jacob his backpack. She watched her son while Thomas left, his cart rumbling along the road. Jacob did not speak for a few minutes, while Thomas left him alone in his thoughts. As they drove, Thomas took the opportunity to speak to Jacob about what his work would be, and the way things were going to progress when he began learning different woodworking techniques.

"At first, you'll be doing a lot of what you already have been. You'll be running errands, fetching water and cleaning the shop. As you learn more and become more competent, you'll learn how to take care of the tools and then how to use them. If we need another set of hands to hold something, you'll do as you're told." Thomas looked around and offered Jacob an instant glance as he looked back at the road. "I know it sounds dull, but it doesn't have to be. We have a good time at the shop. There'll be plenty of time to relax in the evening when all the work is done."

While driving, Thomas pointed out a couple of homes. The majority were grand and luxurious which was larger than the homes Jacob was ever seen in. Thomas was talking about his various projects he'd done to help this family or for that was the case, and Jacob was able to see how happy Thomas was to see his work were eventually being put in beautiful residences. In the future, Jacob hoped to be in a position to design objects that were just as gorgeous and as desirable like the cabinets Thomas Wagner made.

Then, Thomas' wagon was coming towards the workshop and two of apprentices from the past arrived to welcome the apprentices. They shook their heads in respect at Thomas. The one grabbed Jacob's bag, and assisted him in getting out from the wagon. Meanwhile, the second one, who appeared like the one with the most experience took a seat and took over the controls from Thomas. Thomas took off from the wagon. He and Jacob entered the workshop.

Jacob took a look at his surroundings. The store was different to Jacob, now that it had become his place of residence. Thomas told the apprentice that was carrying Jacob's backpack to tell him where Jacob is sleeping. He then was turned towards Jacob. "Elias will show you where things are. Have a good look around and when you get back down we'll talk about how things will work for you here." After that, Thomas walked off through the store. Thomas stopped to take a closer take a look at the work an individual was working on. He then began discussing the work with a young male whom he was observing.

The apprentice patted Jacob upon the shoulder. "Follow me. We have a room in the loft where we stay. It's not large but you will have a bed and a chest for your things. Once we get you settled in, we can come down and get something to eat. The food here isn't fancy but you won't go hungry. Thomas and his wife will see to that." Elias ran ahead of him and Jacob was right behind his steps, attempting to keep pace with him.

"I don't know what Thomas has in mind for you as far as work goes. He hasn't said where he wants you to start out. Most of his apprentices that are close to you in age have already been working for a while and have some familiarity with tools. I suppose that Thomas will watch you and let you work on some things to see what you can do and what you need to learn. But that's up to him to decide how he wants to handle your training."

Elias was able to open a door, and Jacob saw a flight of steps leading to the darkness. Jacob grabbed a lamp from the shelf on his small desk and began the climb up. Jacob followed him around looking around while he went so that the apprentice could remember how to return to his bedroom.

The space located at the top of the stairs was big, though the ceiling was a bit low.

It was clear that the trainees were locked into the ceiling right underneath it. There were about a dozen beds set up each side of the central aisle. Each bed came with a little chest that was at the bottom of the bed. A wash stand was near the end, that contained a basin and a pitcher. The apprentice walked Jacob towards a bed which was near the window. "Your bed is here. The window makes this area cold in the winter so the new boy always gets it. It's tradition. You put your stuff in this chest. Thomas and his wife don't like anything kept under the beds so make sure you don't try to stow anything down there."

Then he continued to explain what was happening within the Wagner family. "There are only two lamps that we can use up here. First boy up here at night brings them up and the last one up here brings them down in the morning. We don't leave them burning here when nobody is around to watch them. Understand?" Elias was looking towards Jacob until he moved his head.

"We get three meals a day. There is always lots of food but the Wagners expect you to come to the table clean and not to waste anything you take." The second apprentice looked towards Jacob for a second. He noticed that Jacob appeared slim and thin. "I doubt I have to tell you to eat all your supper though; you seem like you could use a few good meals."

Jacob was shivering and felt his face becoming hot. Elias was smiling and then hugged Jacob upon the shoulder. "Sorry, I didn't mean to give offense. There's nothing wrong with growing up hungry. I was in your place a few years ago. Being here's a good thing. Thomas and his wife will get you sorted out soon enough. Now, let's leave your stuff, grab the lantern and head back downstairs."

Jacob followed the instructions instructed and followed along with the boy to the bottom of the stairs. They soon returned inside the workshop. Jacob noticed that Thomas was chatting with another apprentice and was showing him a method which he wanted to apply on a certain section of timber. Jacob was laying on his back as he listened to what the colleague was talking about and attempting to take it all into.

After Thomas had finished speaking to the only apprentice, he brought Jacob off and gave him a more detailed explanation about the job Jacob was doing. "Right now, you're going to run errands and clean but when you see me talking with one of the others, I want you to drop what you're doing and come listen in. Listening and watching are good ways for you to learn, especially in the beginning. Once you have been here for a little while and know your way around the shop better I will show you some basic techniques and you can start working." Thomas turned his attention to Jacob. "You need to learn a few basic things before you can start working on your own projects. Once you can start assisting with projects, then we can talk about how much you'll earn and how much of that you want sent home to your mother." Thomas his face softened when he looked at his son. "I know you want to help your mother. Isaac has filled me in on everything that happened with your brother. I want to help you out, Jacob, and I will, but you need to start working and earning your keep before I can do that."

After Jacob smiled to indicate that he had understood, Thomas grinned at him. "I think my wife has been hard at work in the kitchen and it's just about time for supper. Let's start by having you help the other boys clean up and then we can all go in to dinner." Jacob smiled at Thomas as he walked into the kitchen to get started.

April, 1772

Chapter 4: The Tavern

Andrew groaned while standing up straight. He was at a seated position for a time and felt stiff and achy. In the surrounding there were sound of workers and laughing. The sound was pleasant. Thomas was enthralled by the scent of the wood after it was cut, carved and polished He was thrilled to see an object of wood turn stunning when he worked with it. The young man was still learning his fundamental skills, but Thomas was thrilled that he was able to learn so quickly. Jacob learned his craft.

Jacob took a broom, and started to rake wood shavings into a tidy pile. The sawdust occasionally prickled his nose, however today appeared to be good. When he was getting ready to bend over and pick up the heap of shavings and dirt, Jacob was able to hear Thomas calling his name at the front door, which separated the kitchen from the house. Jacob quickly put the dustpan and broom to the side and then headed to look at what Thomas wanted him to accomplish. Jacob has grown old and wiser however, as it was his first apprentice Thomas frequently relied upon Jacob to take care of errands or take on odd jobs.

Jacob didn't mind. It was always enjoyable and exciting to step from the store. Jacob was a fan of transferring items from the shop to different businesses within the vicinity. At this point, Thomas told Jacob to bring a sealed envelope out of his workshop and deliver it to a local pub. He told Jacob to deliver the envelope to the barkeeper and then return to the store. Jacob took a look at the scruffy handwriting on the back of the envelope, and hope that the bartender will be able to identify the person on it.

Jacob took a break from the workshop, and walked along the main street. It was a gorgeous day on the streets. The sun was shining down the streets and the air was so warm that Jacob realized he'd probably sweat before he even got to the pub. While Jacob was walking along the road and saw a line of British soldiers at a corner of the street. The look on his face changed to a grin. Although he was a long time ago and still, he blamed any person dressed in red for the demise of his son. He would always look at the faces of lobsterbacks they saw in the hopes that they would be able to spot someone who killed his father. However, he didn't.

The men he observed for a short time. They stood looking at each other, and not moving. The guys were having fun and laughing over things. Based on the story Jacob could discern that one person was narrating the tale of a fight which he got into together with one colonist. Other soldiers appeared to enjoy the way he argued with the colonist and threatened to take him into custody for creating trouble. The impression was to Jacob that his fellow soldiers seemed to be treating the whole situation as a joke.

Jacob noticed that he'd stared a bit long, when one soldier turned to take a serious expression at his face. Jacob smiled and attempted to be at him in a respectful manner, before rushing to the next street. He could see the soldiers talking and laughing at the soldier as he walked off. He didn't have to wait long to get there, and he sat down to enjoy the cool dark atmosphere as he entered.

A small group of people was seated inside. They had a discussion about the soldiers in the tavern It didn't seem like they were attracted by the red coats. Jacob attempted to not appear like he was listening, however He was intrigued by what they were talking about. They were sharing stories about the things British soldiers have done, and lamenting that fees and taxes had made difficult for them to earn a decent living.

Jacob moved closer. One of the males who was well-dressed and had the appearance of a commander stood up and was speaking to the group. "It seems like you see more and more of those damn British soldiers every day. They seem like they're on every street corner and that every time you try to do anything they poke their nose in where it isn't wanted. I'm an honest businessman. Every time I have a shipment come in they take time going through it, making sure that all the duties and everything have been paid. It's beginning to make it difficult for me to do business." The table was crowded with men who smiled in agreement.

"They keep adding on tariff after tariff and charge after charge. A man can't make a decent profit on anything these days. I swear, it seems like they add an extra charge on if it's the wrong day of the week or if they don't like the look of your face. I've had shipments delayed, goods gone through and damaged while they were being 'inspected', and when I went to speak with one of the customs commissioners, I swear he laughed me right out of his office. I spent hours trying to meet with him only to have him laugh in my face. He told me it was his job to be thorough and that if I didn't like it, I should take it up with His Majesty. He laughed me out of the room." The man turned his head in anger. Jacob noticed the expression on his face as it was red and flushed with frustration.

"Oh, those customs commissioners are the worst. You try to get a clear answer about how much you need to spend on something, and they squirm and talk around the issue. And we just end up paying more, and more, and more for things. Its infuriating. And there is no real way that you can address any issues that you have with them," added another man. He was smartly dressed and had the appearance of a soldier. The men all nodded their heads with approval. They appeared to be all their acquaintances had been in a fight against the British or their representatives at one point or another and were exhausted of it.

"Heaven forbid you have an issue with one of the soldiers or one of their government officials. I've heard horror stories of people who weren't smuggling but who have run afoul of the customs commissioners. Sometimes I think those men are drunk on power and are taking frustrations out on us. They don't want to be here any more than we want them here. Send them back to Britain, I say!"

The table's guests cheered and then began to sing. "Send them back! Send them back!" Jacob experienced a rush of adrenaline through his veins. immediately he longed to be among the people gathered around the table. The table was a group of people who were willing to take action against the men who murdered his brother. He walked closer to find the right people to speak with about joining them and what advice he could give to them.

The bartender saw him and was able to call him out. "Boy! What are you doing in here? Is that a letter I see in your hand? Come here and explain yourself." Jacob was looking around between the barkeep as well as the other men sitting at the table. After that, he reluctantly went towards the bar.

"I was sent here by Thomas Wagner with a letter for you. He told me to give it to you and that you'd know who to pass it on to." Jacob gave the sheet of paper to the person at the bar. He shook his head in a respectful way and turned his gaze towards the group of people who had put down their chants and were engaged in discussion. "Did you need me to wait around and bring word back to my Master about anything?"

The clerk scanned the note and then shook his head. "No, lad, just let him know that the letter got safely into my hands." Jacob looked up at Jacob at the same time, noting how firmly Jacob was looking at the men. "Is something they are saying so interesting, lad? You've been staring and gawking at them since you got in here. Surely it's not just because they were being loud."

Jacob was looking around, and then at the barkeeper. "No, sir. I was just listening to what they were saying and wondering why they were talking like they are." Jacob stared on the ground for a while and tried to figure out the words to describe his thoughts. "They don't... they don't seem to like the British soldiers much." Jacob took a breath for a second. He wasn't sure if he wanted to share something that would make his employer uncomfortable. "I also have some hard feelings against them, Sir. It was interesting to hear what they were saying."

The bartender nodded. "I understand, lad. I do. But you're young still. Keep your head down and your nose clean. Work hard. There will be time enough to get tangled up in all of this when you get older. Now run along and let your Master know that your message got here safe and sound. That's all you should be worrying about for the time being. Do I make myself clear?" The barkeep smirked at Jacob with a smile and the young man smiled to his barkeep. Jacob thought that it would be possible to bring further letters in the bar. He was desperately looking for the motivation to be here to listen to men in the bar were talking about.

After that, he was unable to more wait to leave the tavern. After a moment of sighing, Jacob spun around, ran past the men and walked out on the road for his tiring return trip back to the workshop.

May, 1772

The Sons of Liberty

Jacob turned his lathe on and then sanded off the piece of wood that he'd made into a shape. The temperature was hot in the workshop and Jacob wiped his forehead using the fingers of his hands. Jacob took a look at the surroundings. There were several employees working in the store, despite the fact that it was late in the afternoon. The sun was shining through the shop's doorway and Jacob could feel the dust glinting on the air. He was awed by the place. It was always a familiar scent of sawdust, which gave him the feeling that it was his own home.

Thomas was awed by his hard work Jacob was putting in. Jacob learned the knowledge he had been taught fast. Although Thomas was able to give Jacob numerous errands to complete and tasks to finish but he had the ability to master a variety of fundamental carpentry techniques. Even though Jacob was not getting much opportunity to learn in fine carpentry however, he did manage perform some works on bigger parts. Anything was acceptable in the sense that Jacob is concerned. After he became proficient enough to earn a wage the Master of his company had told Jacob that he'd be able to pay the money back to the mother of his child.

Jacob has been able return to see his mother at least once or twice after he began his training. His mom had found the perfect, but tiny, space and seemed to be enjoying her new home. A little bit of tension and sorrow had started to fade out on her face and she was looking a lot younger. Jacob did not realize the amount of stress was showing up on his mother's face. But as she started to be more relaxed, he was able to see the difference.

He was called back to the tavern numerous times, to hand out notifications and other items for the barkeep. Every occasion he went there was a group of people who were seated at the table. They were often discussing the matter along with those who were British. They changed between times, however, he saw certain faces who became well-known over the course of the course of. The majority of them would be the ones who were actively taking part in conversations, while others watching and nodding in agreement.

It was in the third or fourth visit to the pub that He heard the word "Sons of Liberty" used to refer to the men's group. One of them who talked the most frequently was composing a paper. Jacob was unable to comprehend the content of the document but he wasn't looking to appear as if he was not being observant, however everyone was focused on their writing and Jacob could get pretty close. The barkeep was gone in the back of the bar and left Jacob to play with himself The boy then took the chance to learn the details of the events taking place at the Tavern.

One of the men was looking up, and he saw Jacob sitting close by. "Hey, boy, I've seen you in here a time or two. You're apprenticing with Thomas Wagner, aren't you?" Jacob smiled. "Thomas has told me about you. Your older brother was killed in the Boston Massacre a few years back wasn't he?" Jacob did a second nod in a hesitant way, not believing that his voice would be heard.

There was a massive voice as thinking about the loss of his brother.

"How do you feel about everything that's been going on, boy?" The man inquired. The other man sitting at the table turned his head at the conversation. "I imagine you'd be pretty angry."

Jacob smiled slowly. He was unsure of the best way to reply to him. "To be honest, sir, I've only heard a little about what is going on, but it doesn't sound like the British being here is any kind of good thing for us colonists. I'm mad about my brother, sure. I don't like what I've seen or heard since then, and I think that the British are causing a lot of problems for people. I just don't know what I can do about it." The man sighed. "I'd sure like to find a way, though."

The man sat there and gave him the longest, most curious look. He was just about to speak to Jacob as the barkeeper came back into the main area. He asked Jacob to be there and gave the young man the package. "Take this back to Thomas, boy. Go straight home and don't talk to anyone if you can avoid it. Let him know that Brian said it was important for him to look this over and to keep it quiet if you catch my drift." The bartender patted Jacob to the side before guiding Jacob the way to the Tavern.

Jacob returned back to the workshop. He, according to instructions, gave the parcel directly to Thomas to inform him that Brian handed it over to Thomas. The boss looked at him with a smile. "Good work, Jacob. You've been nice and quick about running this errand for me. Would you like to go and visit your mother today? I have some business in her part of town and it's been a little while since you've visited with her, right?"

Jacob smiled happily. Jacob always enjoyed going to visit his mother. Thomas looked at him with a smile and instructed him to leave to the store and pick up anything he needed to bring. Jacob was smiling and ran off to get the items he wanted to present to his mom. There were a couple of little projects he'd been doing that he wanted to be able to see, as well as a small amount of cash that could be given to her. Soon, he and Thomas were on the wagon heading towards the home of his mother.

They shared the day. Thomas informed Jacob that he'd be waiting with him in the evening, before having dinner and left on the wagon. His mother let Jacob to come in her bedroom where he mingled with her happily about all happening. Jacob was delighted with how content his mom looked after she saw the work that he'd been creating.

"Oh, Jacob, this is all so wonderful. It really looks like you've been working hard and learning skills really quickly. I bet Mr. Wagner must be very pleased with your progress. It seems like your apprenticing there is working out well for everyone." Jacob looked proudly at his mom. He was content because he had made his mother proud.

In the afternoon, Jacob talked more about his activities in the outside of the shop, too. He shared with his mother the story of an apprentice he met and stories of adventures they'd experienced after the day's work was over. He told her how content he was in his home and the arrangements he had made, as well as how they were doing with the food his mother Mrs. Wagner was feeding him along with his fellow apprentices. Jacob then mentioned that Jacob suggested running errands to Thomas and the other men who were inside the Tavern.

As he spoke of the title "Sons of Liberty," his mother sat in silence. Her expression was the anxious face Jacob remembers from the time Samuel was dead. "Jacob, how much have you been doing with that group of men? Have you done anything more than just listen in when you were in the same room with them?"

"No, Mother, I haven't. I mean, I spoke to one of the men and he knew that I was Samuel's brother. He asked me how I felt about the British being here, but other than talking to him that once, I haven't done anything. The barkeep told me to go back to the workshop before I could really talk about much of anything with them."

His mother was relieved. "Promise me, Jacob, that you won't get mixed up with them. I've heard that they are becoming more and more active. Some of them have been arrested for smuggling and for doing things that aren't considered legal. I already lost your brother. I don't need to find out that I've lost you too." Jacob looked up at her. Jacob and her eyes swelled in tears. Jacob blushed in shame.

She spoke about some of some of the actions that the group did. Most of the time, it was about transporting things into and out of harbors within the city. Jacob was unable to comprehend certain things that his mother had to say, however, it seemed like the group were doing actions that created issues for Brits and he was happy about that. A lot of people that he spoken to were known to be a bit irritated about the situation, however when it came down to doing something about it they didn't want to assist. Jacob was aware that being caught would be a disaster yet it was very appealing to contemplate.

He was desperate to get involved, to assist his friends and others that had a difficult time dealing with the British however, he was aware that the mother wouldn't let him know about it. Instead, he dropped his head and looked down at the floor and said nothing. The mom was watching the boy, still concerned about her son's youngest.

"Jacob, please let me know that you will be careful and safe and that you won't do anything that will get you arrested. I need to know that when you are away from me that you will stay safe and keep out of trouble." Jacob did a second nod and his mother dragged him towards her. She embraced him tight. They discussed other topics throughout the time together, however at times Jacob was looking at his mother, he would see her staring at him with a an anxious look on her face.

After a few hours, Thomas arrived with his wagon, and Jacob got on board, getting ready to return. Thomas was looking at his new apprentice. "How was your visit? You look a little worried and that's unusual for you, Jacob. Is everything okay with your mother?"

"Yes sir, everything is okay with her. I was telling her about the group of men that I met at the tavern you keep sending me too. I always hear them talking about things; about how they want to change the way things are here in the city. I told her that I liked that idea. She worries about me that's all. She worries about me getting mixed up in something and getting in trouble." Jacob smiled.

"Well, Jacob, that's something you're going to need to think about carefully before you do anything. You're very young but you won't be young forever.

You simply have to decide what you want to do when you grow up. As for the group in the tavern," Thomas said, Thomas, "it might be best if you don't discuss them to anyone.

They'd probably prefer to keep it private and not let people discuss the plans they're thinking of thinking of." Thomas looked over at his fellow apprentice, looking over his eyes to see the thoughts Jacob had been thinking.

As Jacob lay in sleeping place at night, he turned and turned as he thought about all the things his mother told him the previous day.

June, 1772

Chapter 5: The Plan

The time passed, in the meantime, and Jacob began to make frequent trips to the pub in search of Thomas. It was not often that Jacob or any other apprentices was sent. Every time he travelled to work, there were men. At times, they worked with letters or documents. At other times they would be discussing certain laws being enacted by the Crown regularly. Jacob noticed that he was listening more and paying more attention to the issues the men were debating.

Thomas took on the task of a brand new client. He was constructing an item for a client living in Providence. Jacob was one of the principal workers who created the cabinet even though they didn't have any intricate carving or inlay which was visible on the front. Jacob began to demonstrate the ability to work with delicate materials however, since he'd only just begun, Thomas was able to assign another apprentice to finish the job to create his masterpiece. Jacob was disappointed, however, he was able to understand.

Thomas was certain that Jacob understood the procedure by which the cabinet had to be put together. As it was to travel quite a long distance, it was planned that the cabinet was taken apart so it would fit into the back of a wagon. After it had arrived at its new home, the cabinet was able to be put back together provided that someone was present and knew how the construction method was. Thomas was able to select Jacob to transport the cabinet on its way to its new place of residence. After arriving,

Jacob would be responsible to assemble it, and make sure that it all fit exactly.

It was an immense honour and Jacob was in awe when Thomas was able to inform him that he would be the one who would be charged with building the cabinet. "I can't go myself. I need to make sure that someone is here to oversee things in Boston so I am sending you in my place. I have confidence that you are up to the challenge. I also think that there are things about this job that will interest you more than simply building the cabinet."

Thomas gave Jacob instructions. The plan was for him to head to the Tavern that evening to inform the customer that everything was set to be taken care of. "Ask the barkeep to speak with John Brown. He is the man who has commissioned the cabinet, and it's him that you will be traveling with. He's at the tavern as he has been staying in Boston for a few days while conducting some other business. When the cabinet is all assembled, he will give you a horse to ride back."

Jacob did not hesitate to nod and listened to everything Thomas stated. Jacob was proud and honoured to know that Thomas would trust him with the magnitude of his task.

On the day of cabinet delivery Thomas told Jacob, "Now, the client that you are meeting is at the tavern. Go down there and ask for John Brown. You'll likely recognize him. He's one of the fellows that you have seen meeting there. Let him know that everything is ready and that you will be travelling with him. Once you've let him know, come back and start getting ready to leave in the morning. I expect you'll be gone a few days."

Jacob believed that he floated on the air while walking towards the pub. He walked with a relaxed pace and he feared that the soldiers would seize and inquire about people when they seemed to were being suspicious. One of the last things Jacob would like was for anyone to hinder the task which Thomas was entrusted with. The tavern was open in excellent time, pulled the door wide and went to the inside.

He had grown accustomed to it having a lot of empty space during the day. The people who greeted him as his entrance was unusual. The table at which the men typically gathered was picked over by a group of people, and Jacob was looking around the crowd for someone he knew. The room was dark that area and Jacob struggled to spot anyone who was familiar to him. Bartenders, too Brian is nowhere to be found.

Then, when Jacob began to get nervous, a girl emerged from in the back of the bar. Jacob was familiar with her numerous times throughout the years. The girl was Brian's Felicity. They as well as Jacob were friends at various occasions. She had a sharp wit and an easy manner of talking that Jacob enjoyed a great deal. Her father didn't seem to have any issues with Jacob having a chat with his daughter as well.

Felicity offered Jacob her usual timid smile before taking Jacob's hand. "Jacob, we've been expecting you. Dad's just in one of the private rooms at the back. He asked me to keep an eye out for you. Mister Brown is back there too. They said likely you'd be coming to speak with him one of these days."

Jacob Let Felicity take him to a entrance, into a hallway and then through another door. He felt a little shocked. He was unaware that there were rooms in the back. True, the restaurant was situated in a massive space, but Jacob believed that other rooms were used as areas for lodgers as well as one private home for the barkeep as well as his family. Jacob felt somewhat foolish when Felicity took him into the heart of the pub.

As Jacob entered the room behind him He could understand the reason why they had decided for their conversations to be held in an intimate location. The table was large within the room, and it was covered in map of the surrounding area. Also, there were reports and charts. People were staring at them, and debating the timing and schedules. Jacob was standing in the doorway in a state of confusion and disorientated.

"She always lands in the same cove every time. I say that's a mistake." An elegantly dressed man addressed the crowd. He waved at the map as well as a document which looked like it could be a log of cargo from a ship. "Soon the Brits are going to catch on to her and then everything will be over. If they catch the packet boat while she's going back and forth she's going to be in trouble. A few men in a boat with muskets won't be enough to keep the Brits away, and we need what the Hannah is bringing back this time. We need to do something to help. We need to be there to meet her so that the men get away scot free."

Felicity leant over, and whispered slowly in Jacob's ears. "That man there, the one who's talking. That's Mister Brown. He's the man you've come to meet up with. If you wait around, he'll be happy to talk with you once they've done talking about their next big plan." The girl looked at Jacob. "I have to head back out to keep my eye on the front of the house. I do hope I'll see you though before you leave." Jacob looked at her with a smile when she left.

Jacob took note of what they were thinking about. It appeared that they would like to have them on hand to assist when Hannah reached land with a few products that some men in the group had been trying to get into. Many of the goods weren't harmful, but Jacob was aware that a lot were laden with high duty that needed to be paid before they arrived. This was why people who smuggled them were always trying to gain access by smuggling them.

Jacob experienced a rush of excitement through his body. It was thrilling to think about it that it could be a sure method of retaliating against the British. This wouldn't be able to bring the brother back but it might make the feeling that he'd won at the very least a part victory over the individuals who killed his father and made life difficult for his family and friends. He was eager to be participant in what was going on. He sat quietly, listening and awaiting the opportunity to offer his assistance.

It happened quickly enough. One man glanced at the sky and was able to see Jacob. He looked at Jacob and came over to Jacob. "You're Jacob, right? You're apprenticed to Thomas Wagner?" Jacob smiled as the man smiled. "Excellent. I assume that you're here to tell me that my cabinet is done? If so, we can leave in the morning." Jacob offered Jacob his serious gaze. "I see that you've been watching our plans for the Hannah pretty closely. Should I assume you're interested in taking part?"

Jacob considered his thoughts about. He'd wanted to accomplish something for a long time. He was aware that if he decided to do this it could be very difficult to come back. He was thinking about his mom and how she begged and asked the man to remain away from everything. The thought sparked in his mind what could occur to her if is arrested and convicted or worse was if he wound up in the same way as his brother. He was aware that this could kill the mother of his child, which would could hurt him in a way was not what he expected.

The man was staring at Jacob. "I've seen you coming in to this tavern doing errands for Thomas. I've seen the look on your face. You hate the Brits as much as we do. How could you not after what they did to your brother? Jacob, we need you. If you've ever wanted to join our group before, if you've ever wanted to help strike back at the British, now is your chance. We need extra people to make sure that this will work out and be a success."

Jacob felt torn. He was desperate to aid those who were the Sons of Liberty. He had to be able to believe the impact of his actions with definite results. He put his shoulders in a square and stared at John directly in the eyes.

"I'm in."

June 9, 1772

Chapter 6: The Gaspee Affair

Jacob looked slack and attempted to fall asleep when John Brown's car roared across the highway. The cabinet was loaded in the bed that night prior to. After Jacob was back from the pub, he along with another of the boys carefully removed it from the wall and wrapped every part in thick blankets. Then they layered oilcloth to cover the top. The month of June was upon us and there was still the few days of rain to be enjoyed. What nobody wanted was to have rain ruin the look of the wood or cause wood to be warped.

The front panels looked breathtaking. They certainly made Seamus the young apprentice who created them, the title of a skilled woodworker. Jacob was running his fingers across the smooth surface the wooden piece and had been hoping to one day attain the same level of skill like Seamus was.

The wagon was towed into the workshop to ensure it would be able to sit for the night and be completely dry. John Brown brought it by at night, when he was done at the local tavern. Thomas and Thomas took a long time discussing the cabinet after which the two went to Thomas the home of Thomas. Then, after a few minutes, John came back out and instructed Jacob that he should be prepared for departure at dawn, since the journey to Providence will likely require several hours to finish.

The next day, Thomas took Jacob aside and presented him with a large amount with money that he was able to employ horses to return to Boston. Jacob looked at Jacob and had a look that was unreadable at his face. "I know you've been talking with John and the other Sons of Liberty. I know they meet at the tavern. They have something planned."

As Jacob was trying to speak, Thomas held up his hand. "No, no, I don't want to know the details. The fewer people who do, the better. I know that you're planning to be involved. If you take a little longer getting back here than was originally planned that's okay." Jacob looked up at Jacob with pride and love with his eyes. "Just make sure you come back, Jacob. I owe your mother that much, at least." Then he returned to the workshop and went out. Jacob got up on the wheel and, when John made a cluck to his horses and released their reins dragged off onto the street.

The first time, Jacob could hardly contain the excitement. Jacob had never been to

Boston before and it was thrilling watching the landscape slide across the landscape. As the drive was progressing and the days continued to pass, Jacob found himself growing more and more discontented. Jacob sat down with John on the phone about living was like in Providence was like as well as the things John was doing for a living. He learned that John was among the most prominent business executives of Providence, Rhode Island. He was hit very hard by the tax and tariffs that the British were imposing and was looking for an avenue to fight.

The wagon was accelerating, John explained the finer particulars of the strategy to Jacob. The idea was to abandon the wagon in a safe place and continue on with just horses, until they got to the spot that they were planning to meet with Hannah. The boats would be waiting in order that they could set sail to assist any way required. The British were planning to conduct a patrol along the coast, in order to stop smuggling which was taking place, as well as a few vessels had been confiscated from the British.

At the moment at which they had to leave the wagon Jacob was incredibly exuberant and anxious. Jacob walked out of the wagon, and looked at his horse with a face of fear. "Have you ridden before?" John asked. John looking at Jacob in a face that was hard to read in his eyes.

"No Sir, I've really only ridden on a wagon or walked. There wasn't much call for me to ride a horse in Boston itself and my family didn't have the money to pay for horses when I was younger. But I'm young and healthy and I'm a fast learner," Jacob said. Jacob eager to not get left behind now. John was looking at the man in his youth. It was apparent that he was contemplating things within his head. At last, John sighed and handed Jacob the reins over to some of his horses.

"I hope you're a fast learner. We don't have time to go slow just so you can learn the finer points of staying on the back of a horse." John was able to get onto the horse and sat back as Jacob also did the same. The process took two before Jacob stood on high point of his horse, and was guiding John anxiously as he walked down the road. The horse, thankfully, was calm and had the smoothest gait. Soon it was possible move it from trotting to canter, and the two began to go at a good pace.

They soon could observe the coastline out in the distance. With each step they saw the rowboat moored along the shore. There was a crowd of old boys and men watching the vessel. They were excited when they were able to see Jacob and John walking towards their boat. When they got removed from the saddle and their horses were in place, John introduce Jacob to several of the Sons of Liberty. Jacob was greeted with a warm, joyous feeling when they clapped Jacob on the side as they made him feel welcomed.

A man then looked out over the bay. "Look," he cried with excitement, "the ship has run over the sand! The ship was in pursuit of the Hannah however she managed to beat them out of the water and the British ship is lost!" The men cheered as Jacob joined in. Jacob looked from man to man trying to determine what would be the next steps.

John declared his opinion. "Grab the oars boys! We're going to row out and burn that damn ship to the ground. We can't let her sit there. This will show those British bastards that we mean business and we're tired of them taxing us!" They let out a high-pitched yell and started pushing the ship into the sea.

Jacob was in the boat along with the others and pulled an the oar. When John stood at the bow of the boat, and yelled for the rowers, Jacob thought for a moment about how aching it would get him. He'd never traveled as many miles in a wagon before and had never rode horses, and was in the middle of rowing his entire life. His muscles were tightening up as he tried to row as vigorously and as fast as he was able to.

The sea spray sprayed his face. Before long, the lips and eyes were in pain due to the salt.

When they were rowing and John gave the men's rowing speed for them to follow, a second person named Abraham had been discussing the things could do once they were onto the ship. "It won't be enough to board her and take what we want. That won't hit the Brits where it hurts. This time we have to hit them hard. That means torching the ship."

John was still calling out for the rowers to come and he nodded in agreement. "If the Brits give us any grief, we have to be prepared to respond with force. We can't simply let them mistreat us the way they have been and then let them off lightly."

The boat got closer to the shore. The rowing became difficult.

The tide was rising and each wave was threatening to pull the rowboat away from the shore. But, soon, they were pulling along the vessel. It was difficult to discern however, it appeared like the word "Gaspee" was written on the sides. After his feet landed on the deck Jacob's heart was pounding as if it was about explode from his chest. The deck was smooth beneath his feet. He surveyed the area, waiting to see what others were up to.

The vessel's crew wasn't huge--just 10 men were present. An officer attempted to get people off the vessel. They heard the imposing British tone, and were furious. Jacob turned around just at the right moment to watch an individual from the Sons of Liberty pull out an assault weapon. Jacob discovered the name of his father was Joseph who was not that much younger that Jacob was. Joseph was pointing the gun at the officer before pulling the trigger. The officer's face changed from a look of disdain and anger, to shock. After that, he fell forward. The deck was where he landed dead.

Following that, the events began rapidly. The crew set an fire on the ship, and then, after they had a good idea that the ship was properly burning, they quickly went back to their boat and headed towards shore. Then, they turned to face the other direction so that they could observe the fire consuming the vessel. Going back towards shore proved simpler as the tide carried their vessel to the beach. When they were on firm surface, exhausted soldiers were able to watch as the vessel was smoldering until it got to the surface of the sea.

The crowd roared with excitement from the males. In order not to be at risk of being noticed, the group were dispersed. John and Jacob took off on horses, and headed off on their own and left others to make their own manner. Jacob had exhausted himself and was happy to be able to sit in the wagon and relax during his journey back to John's. The only thing left was to get him back to Thomas his home in the manner he had scheduled and to wait for the outcome.

Winter, 1773

Chapter 7: A Second Massacre Averted

The next few months were filled with activity for Jacob. Jacob continued his training to Thomas Wagner but also became more involved in his group, the Sons of Liberty.

He would spend more and frequenting taverns, in which his gang would meet and speak to the audience, voicing their opinions against the British army or government. A crowd of people would typically begin with a cautious attitude however, as the speakers were able to keep the audience engaged and they began to murmur and grumble to each other in unison. If the audience was warmed up by the roar of ale and a rousing story there would be a few who yelled and smash the tables. It appeared to be getting simpler and easier to get everyone fired up.

The other day, Jacob was in the market and John Brown's voice came exuberantly blaring out at the crowd. The colonists that were listening were extremely agitated as was a group of soldiers who was walking through during the moment.

The colonists walked back and looked at their soldiers they started to drive them into the ground. The whole thing happened in a flash. Jacob noticed himself being pulled ahead as the crowd swarmed those in colorful red jackets.

A few colonists picked up boulders while others searched for lumps of mud that they could throw. They were taken by surprise when they saw around twenty individuals suddenly rushing towards them. They began making announcements and tried to organize the soldiers. They were disciplined and it took only a few minutes for them to stand up against the agitated crowd.

Jacob noticed his palms beginning to sweat when he noticed the soldiers making their muskets ready for shoot. That was the way Samuel had passed away in the arms of a group of extremely nervous soldiers who confronted a raging crowd. The troop was more coordinated than the one Samuel encountered.

Instead of randomly firing into an entire crowd, this commander ordered his troops to be prepared for firing. Muskets were fired with care and the gunmen appeared more secure after paying attention to the commands.

The police officer came forward and spoke to the group. "I don't want to have to give the order to shoot you," the officer stated, his voice breaking clear. "If you disperse and go home nothing bad will happen to you. If you persist in this course of action, I assure you that we are quite prepared to fire into the crowd. We don't want to, but we will if threatened." The officer moved around, muttering in a way that the whole crowd could listen to what he had been speaking.

The people began to talk and glance at one another. The officer continued talking and trying to calm those in the group and bring them to calm. He made no fast moves, didn't act afraid. As time passed, the roaring rhetoric which had got the crowd excited began to dissipate slowly, and then one at a time the group began to fall apart. Jacob exhaled a deep breath that he did not realize the depth of his breath was. He was shaking after he walked off from the place where the mob's hideout had stood. He thought about the different it could have turned out if this officer had been responsible for the soldiers at the time the massacre took place just a few years before. Jacob knew that the final outcome was very different.

The next day, Jacob had the chance to visit his mom. He was averse to her because he'd assisted in helping with the Sons of Liberty burn the Gaspee. Jacob knew his mom did not approve. She had pleaded with him not to be involved with the activities of the group performing however Jacob was aware that she'd be disappointed when she found that he'd violated the advice of her. Now, things have gone to the point that he could not conceal his involvement any longer. He was required to inform her know about the situation.

Thomas gave him permission to leave. Thomas to depart for the day. He could travel riding on a horse, so it took shorter time to travel across the town than had he been walking. He got off the horse, tacked the horse to a fence and walked up to his mother's front door. He felt nervous. He was aware that talking to her what he'd done could cause her to break her heart. It was a horrible emotion. After realizing he couldn't keep it from happening any longer and he rang the door. He waited patiently for his mother's response.

As she walked in the door, and saw Jacob sitting there, her face was ablaze. Jacob realized that he had not been able to see her often enough as he could have, and was feeling guilty for this. His mother appeared older than she did in his memory as a child, and Jacob thought his story will make her appear older. He smiled to his mom while she embraced him, embracing him tightly.

"Jacob! I can't believe you're here! I've missed you. Come in! Come in! I'd love to make you a cup of coffee. I switched from tea. It's different but I'm getting used to the taste. " Jacob's mom took him by the arm and led him inside her house. Jacob looked at the surroundings. It was neat and comfy however it was extremely tiny. But, she'd purchased some new items for her apartment. She was not battling for cash as she was previously. He was aware that his earnings have helped her and brought him joy.

Her house was a pleasant one and tidy like the pin. Jacob's mom had always taken great pride in keeping her home clean and this was not changed with her humble living space. A clean and tidy quilt lay on the bed. The floors were neatly cleaned with a clean sweep, and there wasn't an unclean cobweb visible. The bed was in one corner, as well as a tiny counter, a cupboard an open fireplace, as well as tables. The chairs were hung by walls with pegs and Jacob was able to take two and set them up as his mom walked around the space.

She dragged herself around the fireplace while making coffee. Jacob looked on, pleased to see her look happy and content. He longed to see her but felt more and more guilty for not having visited her more often than would have been the case. It was finally prepared, and she picked a small box of cookies from the cabinet as well. She put the coffee in two cups before sitting with him at her little table. "Jacob, tell me, what have you been doing for and learning from Mister Wagner?"

"Oh Mother, it's been fantastic. I've learned so much. I'm doing a lot of the assembly work for the larger pieces, and he's been showing me some carving techniques as well. He says I'm a hard worker and a fast learner so I am pleased. I even was sent on a trip to Providence for Thomas so that I could assemble a cabinet in one of his client's homes. That was amazing. I'd never been out of Boston before, Mother. I got to ride horses and see the countryside."

"Oh Jacob, I'm so happy to hear that. What do you do in your spare time? Have you made any friends with the other apprentices? I know that Samuel had, and you said that all the ones you work with are getting on rather well. Is that still working out? Surely you don't just eat, work, and sleep do you?"

"No, Mother, the other apprentices and I get along quite well. I've been meeting some friends down at a tavern as well sometimes." His mother smiled and Jacob was a little flushed. He took a deep breath. "Mother, I know that you asked me not to get tangled up in all the revolutionary stuff that's been going on. I know you asked me to avoid getting mixed up with them, but I couldn't avoid it. I need to do something Mother. I can't just let Samuel's death go without there being any consequences."

His mother became stiff. He could tell by the look on her expression she was attempting to remain calm. "Jacob, I'm devastated to hear that. Simply devastated. Losing your brother almost killed me. Everything started when he got involved in all that patriot business. He was in the wrong place at the wrong time, and it ended up with him dying. Now I hear you're mixed up in it, too. It breaks my heart, Jacob, it just breaks my heart."

"Mother, I'm not going to get killed. I promise. Why can't you see that doing this is important? And it's not just important for me, it's important for all of us! We can't just continue living under the yoke of the British crown! Not so far away! Not when they treat us like they do." Jacob got in his seat. He looked through the room, wavering his arms. "I've been doing this for some time and nothing bad has happened to me. It's not going to. I have to help my friends and my countrymen, and I'm going to do it whether you approve or not. I'd like your blessing Mother, but regardless of whether you give it to me, I'm going to carry on." He looked at her with a blank stare and her face was red in emotion.

His mother shrugged in a sigh of sadness. "I'm sorry Jacob. I can't give you my blessing. I don't agree with what's been going on and being a revolutionary will only get you arrested--or worse." Her chair was reclining with her hands clenching her coffee cup that she'd made.

"Then we have nothing more to discuss, Mother." Jacob took his coat off put his coffee on the table and left, taking his mother off the table, lying on her back and crying.

Jacob could hear her breaking tears as he released his horse and hopped onto the horse, and rode off towards Thomas the workshop of Thomas.

February, 1773

Chapter 8: An Arrest

When Jacob was about to enter the workshop the workshop was filled with a lot of people congregating around as though they were being watched by someone. Jacob took his horse in and rode off, attempting to keep his distance from the rest of the crowd, so it would be able to see what was going on without getting seen. There were many people in red jackets walking through the work area, but none of the apprentices was around. Jacob did not speak for a while. It was evident that something major was going on. Jacob was unsure exactly what was happening. Jacob was looking around, and he found the post he was able to connect the horse to before he proceeded to determine the issue.

The crowd mumbled exuberantly when some of the men came out from the building. Jacob moved forward for a better view. Thomas appeared to be walking among two British soldiers. Thomas appeared worried and angry. The hands of his were tied to his back and it appeared as if he was in the middle fighting. Another soldier came through the crowd behind him, with an ugly bruise forming beneath his eyes. Thomas' wife appeared to them and wept, asking soldiers to let Thomas leave and then asking what was the reason they took Thomas away.

A soldier spun and slapped her hard across her face. The woman stumbled and fell onto the floor. The people unleashed a rage. Jacob noticed his tension growing. It's one thing to dispute with a man however, to smack the woman in a way that was uncalled to be done. One of the officers, a soldier, stood up and addressed the audience.

"This man has been charged with smuggling, failure to pay duties and import taxes, as well as various other crimes against the Crown. He is being taken away and will await trial for what he has done. We are within our legal rights to detain this man. This should be a peaceful arrest. We urge you to step away and continue with your business. My men are authorized to fire on the crowd, but I assure you we do not wish to do so. Move along. Move along now."

A large crowd continued to moan and never dispersed. Somebody stepped forward and assisted Thomas' wife up to her to her feet. Her tears were still uncontrollable and was moved towards the left and surrounded by the mass of people. "You have no right to treat a good woman like that! Putting your hands on her! You soldiers should be ashamed of yourselves," said one man in the crowd. all the other people shouted in support.

The police officer nodded his head. "The man who struck Mrs. Wagner will be dealt with back at the barracks. For now, let us through. Let us carry out our job. This doesn't need to lead to violence. It is within our rights to detain this man." Thomas looked at those soldiers not involved in the restraining of Thomas. "Ready your weapons and aim them at the crowd, but do not shoot unless I give the order." Then, Jacob found himself facing an armed musket for the third time. Jacob's heart started racing.

He walked back in a slow manner before disappearing to the background. He was not sure if apprentices were also being held also However, he wanted to ensure his absence was as low as feasible. One of his last goals was to be arrested prior to it was possible to inform the others in the Sons of Liberty that this occurred. It was unclear if they'd be able to aid Thomas however, Jacob was determined to make them conscious of the events. The soldiers, fortunately, focused more to ensure that people didn't get and be irritated by a single man who was trying to get away. There were a few people who were looking to get out when weapons were pointed in towards them.

Jacob noticed Thomas looking around the crowd. At once, Thomas spotted Jacob and was looking directly at Jacob. Thomas was looking Thomas at him in the eyes and said "I'll tell the others". Thomas did a little bow of his head. When Jacob was aware that Thomas knew of his plan Thomas tipped his hat to the man he was working for and then backed his way through the crowd.

Jacob returned to his horse, and took it off. He took it out through the busy street, towards the Tavern. He was not sure who would attend that particular day, but it was the only location the thought occurred to him of in which there were other Sons of Liberty might be. He fought against the thought that, having Thomas being detained, he would have none of his work, had no home to reside, and was unsure about what to do. As he walked into the pub, he walked his horse into the stables before heading to the inside.

It was lunchtime and the main dining room was practically completely empty. There wasn't anyone at the normal table. The barkeeper was present, cleaning glasses. "Good day, Brian," Jacob said. Jacob. "I was wondering if any of the usual group is expected here today. I have some news that they would likely find very interesting."

Brian looked up and scampered at a place in the counter. "They aren't here yet but that doesn't mean I'm not expecting them later. You look like you've had a massive shock, lad. What's happened? Why are you here in the middle of a work day without a specific reason? Did you and Thomas have a falling out?"

Jacob shrugged his shoulders. "No, nothing like that. Thomas has been taken by the British soldiers. They're holding him on suspicion of smuggling and failure to pay duties. I had been off visiting my mother and when I got back, I saw them taking him away. I haven't found out what's happened to his wife although I do know they hit her when she tried to prevent the arrest." Jacob smiled deeply.

"Have they started cracking down on people more?"

Brian looked at his feet and sighed. "It's a nasty business, that's for sure. The Brits are enraged that there is so much smuggling and unrest going on. I don't know why they thought this would be easy, but they did. We're simply sticking up for our rights and showing them that we won't simply roll over and take it. They just need to take the hint and go home." Brian sighed heavily. "Problem is, British justice doesn't always work at a fast speed. Oh, if you assault one of them, or if it's their own men that they have to clear it does. But for the rest of us, we can rot in jail indefinitely. If we're locked in cells, we won't be on the streets causing trouble." Brian was looking at Jacob and gave him a smile at his face. "Problem is, with him in jail, there's no place for you to go and no work for you to do. Felicity would have my hide if I didn't at least offer you a place here for a while until things get a little more settled. I need a lad who can help me move heavy things and it would keep you off the streets for now. Interested?"

Jacob was lost for words He just did a nod. He was pondering which place he could sleep in as Thomas' fate was set. He was aware that returning to the house of his mother was not an alternative. There wasn't enough space for him They had also parted in a bad way. In addition, the fact that Thomas was arrested didn't make her believe that joining with the Sons of Liberty was a positive choice. Going to the Tavern, but, it's definitely the best alternative. For one thing was the fact that it meant he'd be in a position to get a better view of Felicity.

"Okay, I'd wait a bit and then go back to get your things. You're also going to need to return that horse, too. If the Brits start going through all of his things, they will wonder where it went. The last thing you need is to get hauled in for horse theft over a horse you didn't actually steal. In the meantime why don't you head through the door and go find my daughter. She can get you some lunch and find a place for you until we can get things properly sorted out. Sound good?"

Jacob acknowledged his thanks. "Thank you, Brian. I can't tell you how much this means to me. I'll work hard for you while I'm here which I hope isn't for long. You won't regret taking me in."

Brian smiled and smiled and waved Jacob away. "I know you'll work hard, lad. I'll make sure of it." He smiled at Jacob while the boy walked towards the back of the house to search for Felicity. Jacob was hoping that some one from The Sons of Liberty would arrive in the near future so that he could get started spreading the word about what had transpired to Thomas. In order to decide the next move to take be, he'd need return to the place of work and meet with anyone who was around.

He had to communicate with an individual to find out the best approach to ask about Thomas' destiny. The idea of bringing someone back to the same spot was appealing However, he felt this would be a dangerous route. He was not sure what Jacob would like to do was to make someone get in trouble due to his fear to expose his own face. Jacob was thinking about the likelihood to have someone to identify him as a member members of the Sons of Liberty. Jacob knew that should the Brits found out that he was a one of them and they wanted to take him into custody and even have a conversation with him.

May, 1773

Chapter 9: The Tea Act

Jacob and Felicity strolled through the streets, heading to the market. Felicity was required to talk with the butcher who supplied much of the meat used in the Tavern. Normally, the butcher delivers items at the same date each week, but this time, nothing was delivered. Brian requested his daughter, who was appointed the head of the kitchen to visit and talk with him as well, and Jacob has offered to accompany her. The majority the population of Boston was still roiled with fury following the release of the Townshend letters. Brian admitted to being concerned about his daughter heading out on the streets by herself.

Jacob was happy that he got to be with Felicity free of working. It was initially a bit strange being in the exact household with Felicity. The two were always friendly However, as the years progressed, Jacob grew more and more certain that she was the one who he would like to marry. The tavern's life was hectic especially because Jacob continued to work with his fellow members of the Sons of Liberty, and was looking forward to the opportunity to chat with Felicity about his plans to see in their future.

When they were walking along, Jacob kept looking over at the lady at his side. The weather was gorgeous with sunshine and light that highlighted gorgeous highlights on hair. She looked slim and stunning He felt his heart grow larger each time he gazed at her. The couple chatted amiably while they strolled. What a joy it was to know in the fact that Jacob was staying with her and how gorgeous Boston was in summer. She stopped, looked around, and she gave Jacob an uninterested eye.

Jacob recognized that the strange behavior he was displaying. Jacob had tried to appear normal, however, it became increasingly difficult. He knew that if that he revealed to Felicity about what was going through his mind, the rest of his life was going to change. He wanted to take her to court, and then, in the end, get married to her. He'd spoken with her father and been granted permission to talk with Felicity. He understood that Brian was delighted to hear that Jacob would like to stay to be an integral part of his family. All that was left to do was ask Felicity.

"Why are you so quiet?" Felicity was looking at her friend. The way she was normally Jacob was known as a chatterbox. This was among her things she loved the most about Jacob. When they were out together they would always end in laughter and having an unforgettable time. But the day she was with her friend, he seemed strangely silent. She looked at Jacob and was enthralled by his way of blushing as she walked closer to her.

"Felicity, I have something important I want to ask you. We've known each other for a long time now. I care about you a great deal. I'd love to start courting you if you'd have me. I'd make you a good husband, and you're everything I could want in a wife. Will you be willing to court me and see if we would be good together?" He sat in Felicity's gaze in hopes that she'd accept. He was uncomfortable letting his heart out for her. He would usually joke around constantly. He enjoyed having her laugh, however the time was not long enough to share with her what was going through his head.

Felicity looked at Jacob in shock. This was not something she was expecting Jacob to speak. She sat on the floor, and then relaxed her shoulders. "Jacob, I would love nothing more than to be courted by you and eventually become your wife. But I can't let myself love you. Not with the way things are now. I couldn't bear for you to get arrested by the British while you are protesting or doing something illegal. I have heard so many horror stories from my friends, Jacob. I need you to promise that if I say we can court that you will stop doing things against the British and let the lawyers make the changes instead."

It was now Jacob's turn to experience shock. He looked up at Felicity. "What do you mean? I thought you were excited and happy that we were finally doing things to make the Brits pay for all the unfair things they are doing? I thought you wanted us to take the Colonies back and be in charge of our own lives for once. You always have such great ideas for ways that we could protest. Now I find out that you don't want that. Felicity, what am I supposed to think?"

Felicity stared at the man. "I understand why you are so passionate about the struggle. I know what happened to your brother and to the man that you were apprenticing to. When you were just my friend, it was okay. I could accept it. I didn't have to picture what my future would be like if I lost you. If we court, and if we marry, then I have to picture what my life would look like without you in it. I don't like the way that looks, Jacob."

"Felicity, I understand why you're afraid. I don't like the way my life looks without you in it either. But this is important to me, Felicity. You know what happened to my brother. I know you do. Can't you see why it is so important for me to fight to make sure that other people aren't treated badly or gunned down in the street because they don't agree with what Britain is doing? Don't you see why it is so important for us to have our liberty?"

Felicity smiled as she looked at the floor. Jacob knew that she was trying to select her words wisely. "Jacob, I know what happened to your brother was a terrible thing. We all remember the massacre and how it changed everything. I'm mad about things too. But I feel like you are thinking more about the past and that ghosts are more important to you than I am. I don't like that feeling."

Jacob tried to reach out to the girl, but she pulled away and began walking down the road. "I'm not saying no, Jacob. I'm saying I need to think about it and you need to think about whether your past or your future is the most important thing." Jacob stood and watched her leave, continued to follow her as she tried to decide the right words to use.

Soon they returned to talking the same way as they did before. Jacob was delighted with the fact that Felicity continued to show respect for him in the same manner as she had prior to the announcement. In the course of a few minutes it became apparent that he could have fun with her also, even though he often found him thinking of her ultimatum time and time.

The marketplace area in which the butcher's shop was was extremely busy, much higher than usual. While walking along, Jacob noticed that a huge crowd had gathered at the front of the shop which sold dry goods. Some papers were displayed in the windows and people were staring at them, and were talking enthusiastically. Felicity approached one woman and inquired about what it was all about.

The woman shook her head and began to talk about what had happened when Jacob approached the pair. "The British passed the Tea Act. The price for tea has gone way down but only tea from the East India Company. There are a lot of people who are angry about this. We're all just so tired of the rules being changed and then changed and then changed again. When will they start thinking about what's best for us instead of what's best for them?"

Felicity smiled at the lady and, within a short time her and Jacob started to walk down the streets again. Felicity was quiet, and Jacob observed that she glanced at him at times. Jacob wished he could understand the thoughts she was having. He felt like that he could tell. The woman appeared to be looking forward to seeing what her reaction to the information they discovered just now was going to be. Jacob wanted to hurry back to the tavern in order to learn the plans of the group to do in response to the news however he was unable to resist his urge. He was sure that if he went back to the pub Felicity was likely to think that his fellow Sons of Liberty were more significant to him than she did at all, and that was not what Jacob wanted her to be thinking.

They made it to the butcher's shop, and Jacob observed Felicity in awe while she confronted the owner. He was impressed by how strong she was, and also her ability to convince him of the apology of him over his failure to take his father's restaurant the day before. They devised a plan to ensure that every item needed to be delivered to the pub in time, and she managed to get lower rates for the products. Jacob realized that he was in need of Felicity to live his life and that he must figure out a way of making both parts of his life to work.

It was soon the time to go back to the Tavern. After they had walked about two-thirds of the way, Jacob stopped Felicity and turned to her. "I've been thinking about what you said and I understand why you feel the way you do. I can't just quit, not all of a sudden and not today. Please, Felicity, I need to fight for this country. I promise to find a way to do it so that I'm not in danger though.

I promise. Let me try to find a way to do this and tell me that you'll wait while I am figuring everything out."

His heart stopped as he waited for an response. He didn't know what she might respond to. The response she gave could go one way or another, but Jacob was certain of what she would say.

The man was delighted by the time Felicity smiled and entered his arms. "God help me Jacob Maverick, I must be crazy. I'll give you time to figure things out, but you have to realize that I can't wait forever. I can't wait forever."

June, 1773

Chapter 10: The Hutchinson Letters

Jacob could hear the sound out in the streets, even though it was through the thick doors of the Tavern. The sound was that of boots colliding at the foot of the front steps. In a moment the door opened and several familiar faces made their way to the main area. They were Benjamin Edes, John Hancock and Joseph Warren, followed by some of the others from the Sons of Liberty. They were carrying copies Boston Gazette. Boston Gazette and each of them had a hostile look on their faces.

"I imagine it won't be long before the riots start. I can't see how anyone could sit still and accept this," stated Benjamin. "This proves, beyond a shadow of a doubt, that the people who are supposed to lead us and help us flourish are doing the exact opposite! How dare he call for our rights to be taken away! How dare he call it a great evil for us to have more rights!" He took a seat at a table, and looked across the room. His face was red from fury.

"Well, I know that this sure isn't going to make the Governor very popular with the people," Joseph said. Joseph. "We've always suspected that he didn't have our best interests at heart and this is proof of that. I just wish that I could see the expressions on their faces when they realize that all of this has been put out in public for everyone to see. It's going to be madness out on the streets before much longer." Jacob also sat down in his chair, sat down. He then glanced over at Jacob. "Are you ready for things to get very, very serious lad? People can't make up excuses for what has been happening any longer. I think this might be the moment we have been hoping and praying for."

Jacob smiled. He was fed up of awaiting the citizens from Boston to get over their unhappy and act. There was only a certain amount that they and the Sons of Liberty could do without the backing of citizens, and they generally was afraid to do anything. They were a joy to throw dirt and rocks at the troopers, but when guns were fired or other actions had that needed to be accomplished, supporters were hard to find. The feeling was that regardless of the amount they tried to get people excited, the fireworks were always a washout. It was frustrating.

Jacob was sure everyone took a drink before he headed to the location of Brian. Brian was behind, setting up barrels of ale along with other beverages so they were ready for the evening ahead. Brian was looking up at Jacob. He wasn't aware of the most recent news however, he could see that Jacob's young worker was enthusiastic over something. Governor of the city and fanatic, Thomas Hutchinson, had been reported to Britain in order to request that more British troops be sent to Boston in order to thwart the growing rebellion. The Gazette received the letters and printed their contents in the newspaper of the day.

"Brian, I think something massive is about to happen. I have a feeling that the Sons of Liberty will be planning something big. The day has finally come for more action. I think this is the chance I have been waiting for. I can avenge Samuel's death and help get back at the Brits for what they did to Thomas Wagner. He's still in jail waiting for them to decide when they'll try him. I'm tired of sitting here and not doing anything worthwhile."

Brian said a sigh. "I'd show them to the back room again, then. The last thing any of you need is for your plans to be overheard. I would be willing to bet that there are some Loyalists out there who will disagree with whatever you're planning and would like nothing more than to tip the Brits off about what is coming up." Jacob acknowledged, recognizing the information Brian said was not exaggerated. He walked back into the main area and noticed there were other people in the room too. Samuel Adams was now there along with his fellow members He was talking with the men around him with loud, angry voices.

"I always knew that man was up to no good but could never prove it! This is the proof I needed! Now I have that man right where I want him. He's been exposed as the two-faced snake I always knew he was. Now, we find a way to drag him out into the public eye and punish him for the terrible way he allows the British to treat us."

The evening progressed and men began to gather in the back of the room the tensions grew. Then, a man rushed into the area. "Come quick! Come quick! There's a protest! A crowd just went past the tavern! They're carrying a figure that I think is supposed to be that bastard Hutchinson! They said they're going to burn it!" The moment he said his last sentence the man turned and ran back to the front door. The remainder of the crowd was quick to follow.

The crowd was certainly there which was growing with each step. There was a flurry of people in the streets and observing the men carrying the image of Thomas Hutchinson. Jacob looked at someone present within the crowd. "What's happening? Where are you headed?"

"We're headed to Boston Green. We're going to burn Thomas Hutchinson. The Brits have to sit up and take notice of the fact that we won't be pushed down any more! This is the final straw. We won't be lied to and held back any more!" The crowd in the vicinity of Jacob were roaring in agreement and the guy he'd talked to left across the street.

Jacob looked at a few of his buddies. "Do you know what this means? When the troops are distracted with Boston Green, we can go and do something else. Let's hurt Hutchinson in a way that he can't ignore!" Jacob was feeling a familiar sensation pass through his mind. The situation was reaching a point. Jacob became enthralled by an idea. "Let's rob him and then burn Hutchinson's house down. Burn him out and send him back to Britain!"

The scheme was devised quickly. Around half dozen men, Jacob among them, went back to the pub to take horses. When they sped off through the night, Jacob could think of only the possibility of revenge. He only wanted to drive the British from his land and return to where they belong. He hoped that they'd arrive quickly enough so that they would be able to take advantage of the game in Boston Green.

They finally arrived at the Hutchinson home. They stopped and slowed at a couple of blocks away from the home, and then walked through the fields the rest of the route. They were in an upscale, beautiful neighborhood of the city and Jacob felt it felt to be out of place when he was walking down the avenues. It was a plan that had been devised in the course of their journey. They decided to begin their journey at the rear of the house and try to steal as much important items as they could on their journey through the house.

While they were leaving the next day, they could use some of the lamps that burned oil to ignite an blaze. In the event of a fire it was the case that the residence of the governor would be destroyed completely, and the governor would have to go back to Britain. They had plans to swiftly move in order they could get into and out within the shortest duration of time. They weren't ready for was the soldiers waiting in line in front of the house.

One of the soldiers glanced upwards as the soldiers came closer. "You there! What are you doing here?" Jacob walked forward, and addressed the crowd of soldiers. Jacob was a bit in anxiety, but he was hopeful they were able to fool and get around the troops.

"We're just on our way home for the evening, Sir. We don't want to be any trouble, I swear Sir." Jacob was able to feel the gaze of soldiers watching his back. He was aware that he appeared at a strange angle. No one of his acquaintances looked as if they belong in the same place. The soldier prayed that he weren't able to detect the discomfort he was feeling. It wasn't so lucky.

Two soldiers came ahead and seized a few members of the group that Jacob was together. "I think you're all up to no good. I think you need to come with us and answer a few questions." Jacob was able to get back up. While one of the soldiers moved into the air and grabbed another of the group, the man started fighting with a violent force. As the Brits all eyes on him and no one else to attempt to capture Jacob. Jacob was back on his horse and headed off with a handful of his companions following, while the others were firmly held by British.

It was a long and silence trip back to the pub. Everyone was concerned. What would their friends that were captured speak about the things they were thinking about? If they were to be revealed they had been part of the Sons of Liberty and those that were captured were forced to reveal their plans Jacob was aware the lives of his friends and freedom was in jeopardy. Jacob knew they could not remain anonymous forever, but the hope was that his participation wouldn't come to public known.

When he arrived at the tavern, the people were back from the blaze at Boston Green. Jacob was seated tiredly as he was listening to the people who were describing what had transpired. "There were hundreds of people there! All crying out for our rights," stated Benjamin Edes. His face was giddy in excitement. "There were too many of us so the Brits couldn't do anything to stop us. They would have liked to try, I could see that for sure, but there wasn't anything they could do. If they had dared open fire on us, we would have swarmed them. They know when they're outmanned. It was glorious! Glorious!"

Jacob was smiling as the celebration lasted into the evening. Jacob might not have been successful in achieving what desired and hoped for, but it was a success nevertheless. The only thing he could do was hope and pray that things would go good for his family and friends.

November, 1773

Chapter 11: Jail

Jacob sat in front of the bar, setting up glasses and other things well. When Felicity was in agreement to bring the courtship of Jacob, Brian had brought his involvement in the family's company. Jacob was learning about the many different aspects which needed to be taken care of. As he helped run a bar, purchasing items and ensuring that the books were balanced distinct from any other job that he'd done previously, Jacob was finding that it was a challenge he loved and was gaining these skills faster than he had thought.

Also, he was trying to avoid being a part of his fellow members of the Sons of Liberty. Although he was still a part of the group for meetings and discussions, he did not spend as much time in the streets, in protest. He resents the fact that his fellow citizens were in the open fighting for the colonial cause when he was inside. But he remained faithful to his pledge to Felicity. His friends went out at night after evening. At times, they came back with fascinating tales of protests they took part in. They also returned with sad faces and spoke quietly when something did not go according to the plan.

Sometime, they weren't back for a while.

These were some of the most difficult night. The majority of the times the people missing had been simply detained. There were a variety of charges, but the majority included sedition, smuggling and smuggling. Some of the men were also charged with serious offenses as well as a handful were also shot as in the process of executing the plans. Jacob discovered who among his acquaintances passed away and which just wounded. He took every step to aid the families irrespective of the incident.

A few days later, he made the decision to travel with Felicity to see his mom. It was quite a while since Jacob was last seen his mom. Jacob was sending regular money to her and sent her notes as well as letters letting her know the state of his life. He'd received a few from her, but was always putting off seeing her. Jacob remembers the look that she had on her face as the time came to leave her home. He was unable to bear the thought about coming home. Was she afraid to meet Jacob?

Then, Jacob knew it was the right time. He was not doing anything with his fellow Sons of Liberty, and the desire was for his mother to get acquainted with his future wife, whom he was hoping to get married. He along with Felicity headed for her residence at the early hours of the next day. It was a beautiful day for them both, and the couple Felicity eagerly anticipated taking a walk in the sunshine.

They strolled along at a fast pace, talking and joking about things they saw as they went. One time, they observed an elderly British officer who was jogging along the hill. He was a bit slender and unfit. Jacob noticed him and drew his attention towards Felicity. At once, the man's jacket fell unbuttoned and flew out from behind. As his hat fell off and he was forced walk back up the hill to pick it up, Jacob found himself laughing with laughter. Felicity soon turned to laughing, too. They were so fixated in watching him that they were unable to focus on the world in the surrounding area.

Just at the moment Jacob was thinking that Felicity was about to fall over with laughter, he heard the hand fall down his arm. It was a soldier. "Laughing at us, are you? Do you think it's funny when a soldier loses part of his uniform? That it's something to laugh at?" Jacob glared at Jacob. He was able to see Felicity in the middle of the room looking pale. She looked as if she was about to break down.

"I'm sorry, sir. Please, forgive me. It was wrong of me to laugh. I'd never mean to be disrespectful, sir. Please, let us just move along. We have somewhere we need to be and we would like to just move along. Please, I'll never laugh at another soldier again." The thought of having to apologize struck Jacob to be forced apologize to a lobsterback but he knew that he needed to in order that the two of them Felicity were able to get themselves out of the mess.

Jacob knew that the soldier wasn't willing to compromise. "I think that there is far too much disrespect coming from you colonists. I think I'm going to let the judge decide whether you can just go free or if you need to be taught a lesson." The soldier pulled his manacles, and secured them to Jacob's wrists, so that the wrists were tucked in front of him.

The soldier turned his attention to Felicity who was watching the entire scene in a wide-eyed stare and her face a little pale. "Miss, I think it would be best if you returned home. In future, I'd watch my tongue a little more when you are out in public. Civility will get you much further than mocking us ever will." Jacob tried to get his attention while the soldier lean into him so that he could speak to him. "If you want your friend to be able to return home a free woman, I'd go quietly. We don't have anything against the idea of arresting women, you know but it would be a shame for her to land in the jail as well."

Jacob put down his struggles and let the man lead him out. He lowered his head to ensure that he could look at Felicity throughout the length of time it was possible. Her expression was a thing which would haunt Jacob throughout the night, while the prisoner was in.

It was said to take a while to get there. It was extremely crowded. clearly, the soldiers were very eager when the process of capturing colonists. Most of the males and women in the prison were individuals who had been involved in demonstrations or found themselves in the wrong spot in the wrong place at the wrong time. They were detained because they had been fighting with soldiers, or not given them what they wanted. Jacob had also met several of his friends who were members of his group, the Sons of Liberty.

After spending about a week after which it was Jacob's chance to appear in court. Jacob had been crammed into the morning in a wagon before he walked down the courthouse. He sat in before a judge and was informed that the charges were for unruly behavior. The trial, as it went, lasted only about a minute. The judge fined him and said that if he managed to pay his debt and was let go. Felicity was in the room to visit the man, but her father wasn't, and it was odd to Jacob.

While walking back to the pub, Jacob wanted to know who Brian was. In his shock, Felicity broke down in tears. "Oh Jacob," she sobbed, "he's been killed. Father's gone! It's not like you were there. Father has passed away and I don't know how to proceed." In a state of grief, Felicity sank to the surface and Jacob kneeled down next to her, trying to soothe her.

When Felicity had enough calm to talk, Jacob managed to get her to share with him the story of what happened. They had been back at the tavern following Jacob was detained and told her father about what had transpired. Brian was able to find out the jail Jacob was in as well as the specific charges. "It might be better if he just cooled his heels for a little while. The charges aren't that serious. I will see what can be done about getting them reduced as much as possible. He will likely just have to pay a fine and then he can come home. Maybe it will help him decide he doesn't want to be a revolutionary after all."

After that, the situation had become more dire. The soldier was at the tavern on the return journey and had had a drink excessive amounts of ale. The soldier had been involved into a dispute with another patrons, and Brian was there to attempt to end the fracas. This was the time her father was stabbed by a soldier who had removed the bayonet from his belt, and then was throwing it about. Brian suffered for around an entire week, before dying in the hospital; the injury was extremely in depth.

Jacob was locked up at the time Felicity was buried with her father. The death of her mother was over and her father was the only thing she was left. She tried running the establishment on her own, however, it was difficult and there was a lot she was unable to do by herself. Then, she discovered that the man who attacked her father was not in jail for the crime.

"Oh Jacob," she wept, "they aren't even going to bring him charges. My father's gone and there will not be trial, or even anything. My time is now ended. My father was the only thing I was left from my family. Now I'm not seeing him anymore. It's a struggle to carry through, Jacob. So, so hard. I'm not sure what is best to accomplish."

Jacob attempted to wrap his arms around the girl and help her. "You have me, you know. I'm here and I want to help you with everything." He felt Felicity struggle within his arms. she finally let him go. He was disgusted by the expression at her eyes.

"Don't you see? You're the last thing I need! I almost lost you once because of your damned hatred for the Brits. I can't have you in my life. I can't risk losing someone else I love because of politics." Felicity stood up and stared at Jacob and a dismayed look in her eyes. "I don't want you coming back in the tavern, Jacob. I don't want you around. If you need a place to sleep, you can sleep in the stables but I can't have you come back. I'm too afraid that I'll lose you just when things are going well."

Jacob wept bitterly as was watching her walk through the streets. His heart felt heavy. He realized she was battling lots of things and was not being rational, however, it hurt profoundly. But, when he looked at the streets he realized there was a chance to take action and lash to the ones who have hurt him repeatedly and repeatedly.

Instead of visiting the Tavern, Jacob wheeled around and went to the house that belonged to Joseph Warren. The doctor was his name and among the Sons of Joseph Warren. Jacob was the most familiar with.

December 16, 1773

Chapter 12: Boston Tea Party

Jacob was greeted at Joseph's house with warm arms. His wife, the doctor's wife, opened the door for him as he approached and, once Jacob was able to identify himself, welcomed the man in immediately. After the doctor had returned in to his room, he with Jacob were seated in a comfortable chair, and Jacob shared with Joseph the events that took place since their last time together. As he informed Joseph about his detention and the passing of Felicity's father Joseph exhaled a sombre breath.

"Well, that would explain why we aren't welcome at the tavern any more. I think poor Felicity has had just about all she can handle of our activities. We've had to find another meeting place, which we were able to do, but it hasn't been easy. The British are beginning to search us out. They're sick and tired of what we are doing."

Jacob was up, and began to walk through the area. He was angry that he'd missed out on this many hours. He could have helped instead of being rotting in jail or trying to win over the woman who might not really want him. He vowed to himself that it would be his turn to join the Sons and, this time was the only thing to stop him from becoming involved. He had nothing to lose.

Joseph offered him a room at his home for a couple of days. After that, he demanded Jacob to take care of the wagon filled with arms as well as powder Rhode Island. The plan was to store weapons in case the moment comes when guns would be needed. Joseph wanted Jacob to help since, as he said, Jacob had been out in action for a long time so that there seemed to be a great likelihood that soldiers wouldn't be able to recognize him or even suspect him.

Jacob discovered that his work along with the daily errands he had been doing were equally exciting and fulfilling. Jacob was aware that a lot of his fellow Sons were in prison, and while he did spend some of his time in prison but his efforts were at all as meaningful as those which others made. Although the Sons mostly engaged with behind-the-scenes events instead of large grand public shows, he determined to have as big as an impression as he was able.

After several months of helping with small tasks and observing how the city's turmoil grew the opportunity arrived that made Jacob's soul sing over with excitement. Then, finally, they would be able take on the British in a direct manner and hit the thing they seem to value the most: their cash.

The ship Dartmouth was at anchor in the harbor. The ship was in the harbor for a while, unloaded. There was a lot of debate in the city about what would happen to the container. The groups of Patriots, such as Sons of Liberty, among them Sons of Liberty, had requested that consignees not to receive tea deliveries in opposition to the Tea Act. However, the consignees of the Dartmouth did not cooperate. The British threatened to take the cargo of the vessel until the duties were paid as well as the tea consignees who resided in the region were refusing to ship the goods back to Britain. The ship was docked in the same place it was and the people concerned was getting increasingly angry.

Then, a couple of weeks later Jacob was at his room at the Old South meeting house, watching the people shouting in a jumble of the best way to deal with the issue. Jacob felt as if he was just in the right place and at the right time and there was nothing that could prevent him from participating or to stop him from taking on the challenge.

"What's the situation with the ship?" was the question asked by Samuel Adams. "Has she cleared the harbor yet?"

Jacob was able to hear a voice echo through the crowd. "No! Governor Hutchinson isn't letting her leave! He says she has to pay her duties or she won't be allowed out! She can't stay or she'll be boarded, and she can't unload because she won't pay the duties!"

A hushed noise filled the air while people chatted excitedly with each other. They were confused and lost on what was to happen. After a while, plans began to form and soon, everyone was racing around, excited to fight back and put an end to the standoff at the harbor. Jacob was among those who yelled the most. He stood up, and addressed the crowd.

"I say we disguise ourselves and row out to the boat! If we seize the tea and dump it overboard, the Brits won't be able to seize it! Damn Hutchinson and his treatment of us colonists! Damn all of this waiting for the courts to come through! Nothing will happen unless we make it happen! We have to take action. We have to do something about this!"

Samuel Adams spoke up again in an effort to quiet the crowd, and to find an answer. "We have been trying and trying to come up with a legal solution. I have just found out, however, that the

Governor is not going to do his part to come up with a peaceful solution to the matter of the Dartmouth" Jacob observed Samuel take a seat, with looking defeated at his face.

Some men began heading towards the exit. Samuel asked them not to leave. "We aren't done here yet, it isn't time to leave. Please, everyone, we must try to see what can be done about the situation!" Jacob was glued for several more minutes hoping that an idea that could be implemented would come out. Jacob wanted to take action and it was true but he also wanted to be sure that his actions was effective. It is possible that they will not have another chance similar to this one.

Then, Samuel could no longer convince people to remain. A lot of people were grumbling under their breaths. One of the men who was standing close to Jacob was looking at Jacob. "You there, young man. Do you want a way to fix this situation and send a clear message that we won't stand for this kind of treatment one moment longer?" Jacob did not answer, but the man glowed at his face.

"Come with us then; we're about to take the matter out of the hands of the politicians and the lawmakers." The man was up to his feet before leaving the venue, Jacob trailing close behind his.

The events were taking place very fast. When they started to walk toward their harbor Jacob was asking the gentleman about what they planned to take. "Why, we're going to destroy the tea, of course. No tea means no duties to pay. Hutchinson looks like an idiot, and we deprive the Brits of some of their money." Jacob smiled at Jacob. "I hope you're willing to see this through to the end, lad. Once we get out on the water, there is no going back."

Jacob Grinned his teeth with the form of a bitter smile. He was determined not to abandoning or resigning. He'd done it enough throughout his entire life, and this time, he was determined to go to whatever he was required to accomplish. As the frigid air rushed across his face Jacob was never more alive.

"We have to disguise ourselves, lad. When we get closer to the harbor, there is going to be someone who has things we can put on. We're going to look like Indians, lad."

"Why are we going to dress as Indians?" Jacob said, looking slightly perplexed. "Why are we putting costumes on before we row out to the boat?" The person he was watching laughed a loud squeal of laughter, then turned to look at the man.

"Just think! We'll be sailing out to the ship and nobody will know who we are! They won't be able to find us after. The Brits will want to hang the lot of us, but they won't be able to tell who we are!" Jacob smiled as he was trying to maintain the speedy the pace his friend was following. Soon, they'd hit the point where there was not returning They stopped in an industrial warehouse, where they picked up costumes and even paint they could put on to disguise their identities.

After that after that, they were soon returning to their journey. Jacob was able to smell the ocean air and know that they were few miles from where they wanted to go. Jacob looked up to observe the masts of vessels bouncing across the sky. Everyone was moving about. Jacob was able to see other people dressed similar to what Jacob was. The entire crowd was heading to the edge of the lake.

Jacob ran more quickly. He was in front of an unmanned row boat waited. The row boat was crowded with men and they were only beginning to put the oars in and begin to row. Jacob was sucked into the lake. The lower and upper legs of his feet were covered in water and the chill of the water hit him fast. The man didn't let it hinder him from. Jacob was able to jump up onto the boat, and then slapped on the side. The excitement of Jacob was nearly excessive to hold. He felt the spray of the waves splashing his face while the ship started to spin to the Dartmouth. The vessel bobbed effortlessly upon the sea. There were many vessels circling her and crew members crowding up and down the deck. Jacob exhaled a sigh of exuberant laughter, then leaned towards the forward direction, encouraging the boat that he was aboard to speed fast, more rapid, speedier.

"The ship!" Jacob exclaimed as his boat sped towards. "Throw us down some ropes, by God," said another man from the row boat. Then a person appeared on the deck, ready to pull the ropes down to ensure that Jacob as well as all the other people could get on board. The deck was filled with different kinds of people. There were British troops, crew members of Dartmouth, crew members from Dartmouth as well as other men who were dressed in Indian costume. Jacob took himself off the rope to the deck, and then began to look at the surroundings to figure out what next move was.

"Heave this over," the voice cried near Jacob's shoulder. He turned to his left and saw a man battling using a wood chest. The chest was clearly marked: Davison, Newman and Co. The chest came from London. With no hesitation, Jacob took the chest, and then threw it to the side of the vessel. He smiled as the chest sank into below the surface however there was not chance to remain in awe for all of. He took chests after chests, tossing them into the water and cheering each whenever he heard the sound of a splash.

While it seemed like an length of time, eventually the vessel became empty of its items. Jacob was able to see the containers in the sea. There were some floating on the water's top while others were gradually sinking. One voice yelled, "I think that's all boys." As soon as the voice was heard, everyone started to run towards the rowboats from where they came.

It was an easy journey back to the shore. While Jacob got up on the shore, he glanced at his shoulders. There was a familiar voice who was cheering him on. It was Felicity. It was clear what he looked like because of his disguise. And she was in support of what he'd performed. Jacob smiled and kissed her and then walked off across the street.

Chapter 13: Epilogue

Jacob walked around the tavern with a feeling of happiness. Then he felt as if it was the same place he had always been.

He was at the pub a few days before the events at the harbor took place. He wanted to allow Felicity enough time to consider whether she was feeling happy or sad after seeing what the men had performed, and also desired time to let the Brits unwind a bit. Governor Hutchinson was out to collect blood during the initial days following the news that tea of the Dartmouth had been found at sea.

The man had opened the tavern's door to the left and looked in. The place was bustling with tables filled and people gathering in the bar. In a brief moment, Jacob found himself looking for Brian and his heart sank slightly when he realized that her father was murdered. Jacob wiped his eyes for a while and returned to looking through the crowd. He didn't have to wait long to locate her.

The front door of the room opened and Jacob was watching as Felicity was seen coming out with an enormous, bulky tray of food. The look on her face was troubled, but she looked beautiful and she walked with a smooth moving walk. He felt his heart pounding when he saw her. He needed to find out how she felt now about him.

Jacob was walking through the tavern, and was heading towards the bar. He was aware that, since Brian not there anymore, Felicity was striving to be everything and that standing in front of the bar could be the best method to attract her focus. It was true, however was not prepared for the response he received. As she saw him his face, Felicity's smile exploded into an enthusiastic smile as she put her arms in his direction. Jacob held her tight, and held her in his arms for a few seconds.

Felicity stood up straight and stared at Jacob. "I'm so sorry for the way I acted. Please come in and stay for a while? I want to talk to you about everything that has happened, but I'm so busy at the moment. Please don't leave before I've had the chance to say my piece." Jacob accepted and sat down and moved out of the way. The rest of the night just watching Felicity while she made her way through the space. Her skills were impressive when it came to running the tavern and he could see that, however He could tell that she was exhausted and a bit stressed.

After the customers returned home stuffed filled with food, beer and good company Felicity got the opportunity to relax in a chair and take a breather. Jacob was able to move over so that he was seated beside her, and was waiting to hear what she would have to have to say.

"Jacob, I saw you taking part in the event in the harbor. Everyone is talking about it, you know. Everyone is saying what a brave thing you did. I agree with them Jacob. I'm sorry I was so afraid. I'm sorry I sent you away. I want you to stay, Jacob, and run the tavern with me. Would you do that?" The woman had stared at him before turning her head was drawn and nervous.

"Felicity, I would love to. I have loved you for a long time and staying here would make me so happy." The two kissed and

Jacob gazed at the space with a sigh of happiness and pride. He truly was home and was happy for the first time after a long struggle for a better existence for his fellow countrymen as well as himself.

The next half one hour Jacob took in the stories regarding the happenings at the harbor and was inspired to walk down the harbor to look it. The tea was sour and had sunk to the bottom of the sea however, there was a scent throughout the air. The vessels were gone, and the only thing he could see was broken wooden boards left from chests that were still floating on the sea. He was looking at the surrounding. No one seemed to be recognizing him. Actually, if you look at their disguises they'd worn it was possible that he struggled to identify many of the people were on the boat with. It appeared like they'd performed something that had everyone -- including the Brits--take note.

Following the days in the days that followed Jacob and Felicity were not actively seeking the latest news about the events but they did hear little about what was going on at the courthouse and the surrounding area of Boston. As they learned concerning the burning of Peggy Stewart the scene was as if the tides been turned around for the best. All were standing up for the rights they'd been denied for a long time.

At times, Jacob would gather with some of the people had shared a boat with. They would sit and talk about the happenings of the night. It was a pleasure to revisit it, the sensation of the sprayed water across their faces as well as the excitement that swept them while they dropped the crates in the sea. Some of the men actually returned. They had told Jacob that they'd paddled around on the boat and travelled all around the harbour to ensure that there was no damage. One thing that they never in mind was to get anything from the ship. All of the cargo had to be destroyed else the gesture would've ended in futility.

Felicity and Jacob settled into a routine life and just a couple of weeks later their first child was born. Their son Adam, who was a healthy baby boy were naming Adam who was just at the age of three, Jacob visited his mom. It was a long time since he last saw her and was worried that something might have been done to her. But the moment he got there she appeared to be in good health and delighted to meet him. As per Felicity's wishes, Jacob and his mother resolved the issue and requested that she come to reside with them, so they Felicity would be able to help their son. Felicity felt increasingly insecure and unable to help herself, and Jacob's mother was like the family they had to be to be around. Jacob's mom was willing to let him relocate to the Tavern and Jacob realized that the right thing to do for her.

Jacob and his mom never talked about their thoughts on Sons of Liberty again. Jacob was aware of how his mother thought and decided not to debate with her over the issue anymore. He had spent enough time with her.

After Adam was first born Jacob was looking down on the new baby with awe. He was certain that he would take every step to make sure that the child was free to grow up in a nation that was not controlled in the manner that it was in the colonies. Felicity noticed his resurgence of passion for the country and though it was a source of concern but she remained calm and was waiting for what the future could bring. There was no time to sit and wait.

Then, when all protests were finished and every attempt at reconciliation did not work, it looked as if the entire country was in war. Felicity was aware of the reports and was not surprised by the sight of Jacob came up to her. Jacob had a tense look at his face, and it was heartbreaking for her. Jacob was hesitant to join the military until was possible. Jacob was part of his fellow members of the Sons of Liberty helping store foods and weapons, as well as moving soldiers from one region to the next. The man noticed that he was separated from his family and friends more and more often, and recognized that he had to decide in order to support with the Patriot cause.

As he realized he was unable to split the time any longer, Jacob knew he had to speak to his wife. Jacob asked his mom to bring Adam off for a short time in order to speak with Felicity and inform her of what he'd decided to do.

"Felicity, I have to see this through. I can't have gone this far and then let others do the rest of the work. It isn't fair. I know that you've heard the rumors and they're true." Jacob had looked over at his wife and noticed her expression when he spoke to her. "I have to sign up, Felicity. I have to do this. Do you understand?" Jacob stood his hand in the air at the thought of what wife would think.

Felicity smiled, but she could feel the tears begin to grow. Her first reaction was to be silent she was not sure if her voice would be able to be heard. As she grew stronger her voice, she smiled at Jacob although it broke her heart. "Jacob, I understand. I know you need to do this, and I won't stand in your way. Just please, whatever you do, try to come home to us as soon as you can."

"I always will, my love, I always will."

www.ingramcontent.com/pod-product-compliance
Lightning Source LLC
Chambersburg PA
CBHW071440080526
44587CB00014B/1922